Leftover People

A Journey Through Post-Rock & Roll America

Brent Jensen
AUTHOR OF *NO SLEEP 'TIL SUDBURY*

EDWARDS PRESS COMPANY
TORONTO

Edwards Press Company

FIRST EDITION

ISBN: 0987715917
ISBN 9780987715913

For Christopher Long, an individual who uses his illusions like no other.

Dramatis Personae

Plenty of bows to be taken this time around.

Steve Flemming, for accompanying me through all of the uncertainty with a consistently brave face and unwavering support. I was lucky to have him. Chris 'The Pink Chief' Long, for enabling this entire adventure. When it was over, he earned my lifelong respect when he said to me, '*don't worry about how I'm portrayed in the book. Just tell a good story.*'

Thanks to author J.M. (*it's a book about rock and roll!*) Blaine, for assuring me that writers don't need to explain anything to anyone; to Martin Popoff, for his kind words and for a crash course in the business of writing; to Lee Eckley, for looking out for me from day one (not to mention introducing me to Lee Aaron); to Ian O'Malley, for being a quality human being and for inspiring me to aim higher without even trying; to Dave Ling and Chuck Klosterman, for their support and contributions towards putting a smile on a small town Canadian kid's face; and to my close friends of many years Liam Ennis and Bryan Sloss, for providing critical input towards the writing of this book. And of course, much love to my dear wife and best friend Alison for her never ending demonstrations of patience.

Massive amounts of appreciation are due the following people for their incredible support and kindness – James & Jenny Wylie, The Sutoski Family, Brad Jemmett, Jim & Jennifer Callahan, Colin Henderson, Kent & Sian Bailey, Brooke & Trevor Dennis, Melissa Flemming, Nancy-Jo Ramsay, Jas Singh & Tara Chetkowski, Rod

O'Connor, Rick 'Teddy' Radovski, Paul Rose, Nicky Wenzel, Larissa Moffatt, Chapters Canada, Sean Kelly, Nick Walsh, Don de Leaumont, FDM, Chad Bowar, Alan Cross, Shawn Macomber, Dawn Lalonde, Laura Stradiotto, Tony & Angie Anselmo, Jesse Long, Jenny Jelen, Parveneh Pessian, Jeff Rozdeba, Wendy Gilmore Nelson, Charles & Lissa Knight, Ty Oglesby, Jack Starr, Todd Kennedy at WFIT-FM, Neil Daniels, Thomas Doyle, Lee Aaron, Darby Mills, and to the unnamed individual responsible for the Spotify *No Sleep 'Til Sudbury* playlist. You did a great job with that.

Prologue

Every single day, human beings send little signals to the rest of the world. Some of these nonverbal signals are blatant, some barely perceptible. These signals are like tiny bread crumb trails; portals into the reality of what these people are at their cores. More telling, of course, when the signal is unintended. As, say, a tattoo often is.

Little things. Like, shoes. Reactive facial expressions. Awareness of reflective surfaces. How clothing is manipulated. Selection of self-representational symbols. Reaction to the presence of a camera. All of these signals are living things that comprise an unspoken network, all part of the map into the heart of the pyramid where the sarcophagus is kept. They tell you everything you need to know. You just have to respect the import of the signal.

One
Brand New Moon

~

Swimmingly is a word I'd used twice in my life, both times in mordant context. But it was the first word that came to mind at that time, seven months ago. I felt almost tempted to use it, because things seemed to be going quite...swimmingly.

The dictionary definition of this word is '*effortlessly, without difficulty; with great success.*' This made it ineligible for use in the context for which I had intended. Really I was happy about this, because swimmingly is an uncomfortable word anyway.

Things were going *well*.

My debut book *No Sleep 'Til Sudbury*, a memoir that invited the reader to take a closer look at the reasons why they listened to hard rock and heavy metal music back in the 1980s, and why they likely still did today, was out there in the world now. Good things were happening. The reviews were positive, and I had received encouraging correspondence from writers I looked up to. I had been getting emails from readers all over the place thanking me for writing the book, and it had taken some time for me to reconcile this concept in my mind because it seemed so crazy. Things I had previously considered to be abstractions were now in fact real. The impact I had braced for upon the book's launch had proven unnecessary. I'd never really been so great at *feeling the love*, but it was there to be felt. Hell, I even made a few new friends.

1

One night as I sifted through emails, I included my spam folder as part of the exploration. I didn't typically do this, as the outcome is predictable. But I'd just returned from a vacation whereupon I had completely unplugged myself from the grid, so I figured I'd at least have a look. The second email I saw in the junk folder was entitled:

Reliving my youth...

Exactly like that, with the ellipsis trailing off to indicate an unfinished thought. I wondered if this vague ideation would reveal itself to be an opportunity to enlarge my penis, or to receive a twelve million dollar wire transfer on behalf of a long-lost and recently-deceased dignitary relative from Kenya. I was tired but not completely humourless at this point, so I opened it up.

Turned out the email was from a chap named Ian O'Malley, an on-air personality at Q104.3 in New York City. In the note, Ian explained that he had noticed a copy of *No Sleep 'Til Sudbury* in the corner of his studio amongst a pile of books. He had only noticed the book because he wondered, in his words, *"Who the fuck would substitute Sudbury for Brooklyn?"* He was also intrigued by the possibility of the book's connection to Ontario; O'Malley would go on to say in his email that he had grown up in eastern Canada. He had also hosted a radio show in New York back in the 80s called "Metal Shop" that played most of the bands featured in *No Sleep 'Til Sudbury*. During this time, he had forged meaningful friendships with some of the members of these bands I had worshipped in my youth.

I sent an email back to O'Malley thanking him for taking the time to reach out. I appreciated it. Then he responded, and I responded to his response. Our email correspondence went back and forth enough times that weekend to elicit some 'bromance' snarkiness from my wife Alison.

At some point later on O'Malley had said he would be in Toronto, so we arranged to get together for a few drinks and some chat. In person, I was not surprised by Ian O'Malley. He presented more or less exactly as I expected he would - engaging, friendly, and full of character. Really nice guy. I liked him immediately. The chat came easy and comfortably, and the drinks flowed. He told hilarious stories, one for every musician I threw at him both popular and obscure. James Hetfield. Nikki Sixx. Bret Michaels. Maybe even Dave Murray. We had a lot of laughs that night, O'Malley and I. Later that summer, Alison and I spent a weekend with him and his family in Connecticut and had an incredible time. We communicate regularly now, and he's a great person I'm fortunate to call a friend. He opened my eyes to a lot of things I hadn't previously seen. Before I did eventually open that initial email in my spam folder, my finger had hovered just above the delete key for at least three seconds, with every intention of striking it. Not sure why I didn't.

Life can be funny this way.

⌒◌

In addition to Mr. O'Malley, plenty of interesting new individuals came into my life via cyberspace during this time. Some of these initial communications furthered themselves into in-person meetings, and then into personal friendships. Some went undeveloped. I've come into contact with all kinds of people as a result of the book's release, and some of the more interesting interactions have occurred at in-store appearances to promote *No Sleep 'Til Sudbury*. It's in this setting that one truly experiences the absolute richness of individuality in all its splendour.

Where else can you hear stories about people leaving $300 Gucci underwear on airplanes, and then denigrating airline staff using the c-bomb upon not being permitted to re-enter to plane to retrieve said undergarment? At book signings, that's where. This environment, the open marketplace of a bookstore, spans a very broad spectrum of human perspective. There are no filters other than those governed by the most basic levels of social decorum, and that ain't saying much. Everybody reads books, or at the very least, looks at the pictures. And some of these people are going to tell you about it whether you like it or not.

At one signing I had done, a normal-enough looking chap approached the table where I sat and nodded solemnly, staring at my book.

"You know any of these people?" he murmured without looking up from the table.

"You mean personally? No, I don't," I said.

"What's the book about then?" he asked tersely.

Then? My mind worked to prepare for the inference that was likely going to be made within the next four minutes.

"The book is about what it was like to experience music from the perspective of a cold, bored small town Canadian kid in the 80s." Not the answer I usually give.

"*Um-hmm.* So you don't know anyone that you write about here."

"Well, I did meet Gene Simmons at a book signing once, and there's a story in the book that details the meeting," I responded.

"Gene Simmons. He operates within a very close-knit circle of elite Jews in Hollywood."

Whoa. Didn't see that coming.

"Uh-huh," I replied.

"That might be considered a racist comment," he obfuscated, looking up first at me, and then turning his head from side to side to scan the store. "But everybody here understands. Everybody is thinking the same thing."

"Um...yeah." I wasn't. Nor did I understand the point he was trying to make. He continued this line of discussion for some time. He was sapping my strength, along with any interest I may have had in engaging him any further.

"I'm going to have a look at your book," he said very matter-of-factly, and reached down for a copy. After sharing his little manifesto with me, a captive audience, I thought this may have been his way of acquiescing and mercifully walking away to the cash register with a book. I took the cap off of my Sharpie, assuming he meant he was going to buy it.

"*No, no, no, no, no,*" he scolded. "I didn't say I was going to *buy* one. I said I was going to *look* at your book."

Man. Usually I find this sort of thing mildly entertaining just based on sheer peculiarity, but now I just wanted Hitler to leave. This wasn't a fucking yard sale. He flipped through the pages with his Gestapo thumbs for what seemed like eight years.

"Thanks," he sniffed. With that, he put the book down, puffed out his chest and sauntered away.

You get all kinds at book signings. There were times when I was made to worry somewhat about my personal safety. At a signing in Toronto, I was encountered by a chap acting very peculiar, who refused to look me in the eye as he stood in front of me perusing a copy of the book. He looked to be maybe mid-thirties. A bit weird looking. Gave off a really creepy vibe. Flipping, flipping through the pages, forward, backward, and forward again. His eyes seemed directed at the pages, but I wondered if he was even seeing them. His chin almost seemed connected to his chest.

"Are you into this kind of music?" I finally asked.

He nodded in the affirmative.

After a few more minutes of page flipping, he finally spoke.

"Have you met Axl Rose?" he asked very quietly.

Here we go.

"No, I haven't," I responded disdainfully. Sometimes I just didn't have the patience for this stuff.

The flipping continued, and then he spoke again.

"Have you ever met Gene Simmons?"

"Yes, I have. At a book signing. He wouldn't remember me."

He stopped flipping.

"Well, I was only looking," he said almost sarcastically, putting the book down and walking away.

Weird enough, but this was only the beginning. For the duration for the appearance, I would see this guy every few minutes in my periphery – just off over to the left of the store looking at a book, or way over to the right thumbing through a magazine. I noticed him looking at me. He averted his eyes each time I looked back at him.

When the appearance ended, I packed up my additional books and posters along with some Sharpies in a box, and left it there to walk over to Starbucks for a coffee before leaving the store. As I walked away I didn't know where my new friend was, but as I stood in line and happened to look back at the signing table from about two hundred feet away, there he was – both hands inside the box, rooting around in it. I started to walk back towards him and he moved away very briskly when he saw me coming. I had no idea what he was doing, or why. I locked the box away in my car and returned to Starbucks.

As I waited for my coffee he was there in the near distance, flipping through a magazine and looking up at me periodically. I wondered how this situation would unfold.

Once I was in my car, I caught a glimpse of him getting into his. As I merged onto the highway on my way home, his white sedan appeared in my rear view mirror. Now this weirdo was following me.

He stayed behind me for a few exits. I considered just pulling over to end this, and as I put on my indicator to change lanes he sped past and exited on the next off ramp. I looked for him at my next in-store appearance, but he didn't appear.

I would learn that this stuff was all part of the whole weird and wonderful gig. It was a first-hand anthropology examination. Sometimes the results were ghastly, and other times they were uplifting. Some interactions left me longing for a HazMat suit, and others inspired me to jump out of my chair and embrace some of the absolutely glorious human beings I was lucky enough to meet.

And all the while, questions were asked of me that never failed to entertain:

"So, did you ever party it up when you were younger?"
"I'm writing my own science-fiction novel. Can you help me with it?"

"Do you own this store?"

(Reading from the back cover of *No Sleep 'Til Sudbury*) *"Rock history and academic treatise...are you an academic?"*

"Are you a weightlifter?"

"Are you a magician?"

"Can you sign our hands?"

Promoting the book on the Internet is a completely different animal.

My online promotional strategy was to reach out to the obvious touchstones that could spread the good word - radio stations and media outlets, music personalities involved with the genre, et cetera. And with the availability of Twitter and Facebook, I could even attempt to get the attention of the musicians themselves - those lofty demi-gods who suddenly appeared to be so much more accessible to me now in the Information Age. These people were the individuals responsible for my writing the book in the first place, so it made sense to throw my hat into that ring. *No Sleep 'Til Sudbury* Twitter and Facebook accounts were set up post haste.

With Twitter, I used to wonder if my account was not working in the way that it should somehow. I reached out directly to plenty of individuals, with zero response. Initially I had started by sending links of articles I had written out to these guys, or I would send the link to the book's website. No answer from anyone. Then I wondered if I had to be more creative on Twitter. I would try to use humour as a device to get some attention. Still nothing.

How these people could not respond to the witty ripostes I was using was beyond me. Some examples:

When Anthrax guitar player Scott Ian used Twitter to auction off some of his autographed guitars, I offered:

"More intriguing than the guitars is the fact that your signature looks like it reads 'SATAN'. You must scare a lot of bank tellers with that".

It's funny, come on. It actually did look like that. No response though.

When Twisted Sister's Dee Snider lamented that he would have to change the lyrics in some of his old songs for inclusion in a musical, I tweeted:

"Burn in Heck?"

This was a lighthearted jab at Twisted Sister's song titled "Burn in Hell" from their *Stay Hungry* record. I cackled as I typed it, thinking *for sure* this tweet would get a response.

Crickets.

The cheeky comments were not limited to musicians. Jerry Seinfeld retweeted an Alec Baldwin tweet saying that percussionists were always in shape. My response:

"Somebody better tell Cheap Trick's Bun E. Carlos"

Zilch responses. Clearly my Tweeter was broken.

But no matter. I may not have been hearing from the big stars themselves, but I was hearing from a lot of people who had lived among them and moved in their private circles. And this was actually even more compelling in most cases, quite honestly. Sometimes in a good way, other times not so good.

I'm still learning to be careful what I wish for. Because while the Internet has certainly made the world a lot smaller for me, the unfortunate trade-off is that my imagination has been condensed considerably in the bargain.

⌒◌

The big thrill for me in the summer of 2012 was being scheduled to appear at Records on Wheels in Sudbury to sign copies of *No Sleep 'Til Sudbury*. I literally grew up in this place, the Vatican of northern Ontario record stores, during my forlorn teenage years. I was pretty stoked about the whole thing. Nervous too. My mind ruminated over the vast possibilities involving any number of random individuals from yesteryear who could have showed up, and what that experience might be like. Turned out none of them did.

I checked my email later that day, and my inbox displayed an unread message from someone with a name unfamiliar to me:

Hi Brent,

I recently discovered NO SLEEP 'TIL SUDBURY online. As a fellow author I recognize the importance of press and as a long time music/entertainment writer/critic, I'd be delighted to review the book.

-Christopher Long

I looked this guy up on the interwebs. I'd heard of the website where he posted his reviews, and his separate personal blogging site advertised him as an '*entertainment and showbiz guru*'. Interesting. My learning curve would continue its upward undulation.

I sent Christopher Long a copy of the book, and he seemed to devour it. We exchanged emails. It was *Christopher* in my first email response, *Chris* in my next. And soon after, jokes and sarcasm without the proviso of smiley faces or exclamation marks. Fast cyberfriends now, Chris Long and I.

All of this stuff was growth for me. *Prosperity*. At every infinitesimal progression that marked the rise of this new thing, I evaluated its architecture. Partly in satisfaction of its development, and partly to detect any form of illusion. As much as I've slipped my small town skin, my guarded naïveté will never really leave me.

Another few weeks of casual back-and-forth with Chris took our exchange into the month of August. Then he sent this email:

------Original Message------
From: Christopher Long
To: Brent Jensen
Sent: Sunday, August 12, 2012 5:18:44 PM
Subject: PROMO

And the #1 reason your book is so flippin' awesome:
You reference Marc Storace AND Lee Aaron in the same story!

As for my inquiry, I simply wanted to discuss and encourage you in perhaps moving forward with a Kindle version of NSTS. Finally, I'd want to entice you with the possibility of a Florida dual author appearance. It's not as crazy as it might seem.

Be sure that none of these are time sensitive issues.

-Chris

For some, this scenario may have resembled the unfolding of a *Dateline* episode. I have to confess that it did for me.

My first inclination upon reading this email was to recoil in immediate dismissal of the idea of travelling to another country and placing my personal safety in the hands of someone I had not yet met in person. Lester Holt and Keith Morrison would have surely agreed with my approach. I took a step back to consider everything I had ascertained thus far about Christopher Long over the brief course of our communications.

The World Wide Web fashioned his life story as that of a pocket-book tragic hero - lead singer in a weird and obnoxious metal/rap-type band based in Florida in the early 90s as a young and increasingly more troubled man. The band bordered on success but never made it. Trouble was proliferated by drugs, alcohol, and women (I'm not making this up). Then, our hero joined hair band Poison's touring organization as bassist Bobby Dall's personal assistant for two of their US summer tour extravaganzas. Much anguish was suffered at the hands of a cruel and insensitive Dall, and Long was forced to remove himself from Poison's employ for fear of a complete mental and physical collapse. Long then wrote a book offering the lurid details of his ordeal with Poison, drawing intense ire from the Poison organization and their fans. More anguish ensued at the thought of having to pull the book at the last minute and face litigation from his publisher. Rock bottom lows were experienced. Then - our protagonist found god, and redemption was his for the taking. A happy ending. At least as far as I knew. These events are all described in colourful detail in Long's two books, *A Shot of Poison* and *C'MON*.

And now this guy, whose online pictures showed him carrying a pink Hanna Montana purse as an accessory and having painted pink nails to match, wanted to sell his books in partnership with *me*.

This was a lot for me to digest.

If I chose to involve myself in this, it would be through defining the upside and the true potential, in the face of all of the obvious things that could dissuade me. And the potential here was that I would be Neil Armstrong, walking on a moon brand new to me.

Observing. Absorbing. Learning. All with a Jesus receiver and former Poison employee as my co-pilot.

Two
Pollyanna

~

------Original Message------
From: Brent Jensen
To: "Christopher Long"
Date: Monday, August 13, 2012 11:51:15 AM GMT-0700
Subject: Re: AUTHOR APPEARANCE

You're an effective salesman, Long. That much is for certain :)

I think this is a great opportunity, and you make some great points. I like the idea of cross-promotion.

Timing isn't great for me at the moment.

Did you have a general timeframe in mind for this appearance?

Now it was Long. Not even Chris anymore. Thick as thieves now in continuing down this path in cyber-lockstep.

And I was being honest. The timing *wasn't* great, based on other commitments I had. I was still weighing the possibilities of this venture - running through the scenarios silently in my head, sometimes verbally with wifey. The timing was actually pretty terrible. If I did go, I would have to push it into the next calendar year. I expressed this to Long, and he advised not to sweat it - as much as he wanted to do it as soon as possible, it wouldn't be a deal breaker.

These flexibilities just fanned the flames. I wasn't being facetious; Long *was* an effective salesman. My impressionability was marvelling at the pictures being painted by this guy. Over time, I talked myself into this trip because I forced myself to believe that the pros usurped any con I could come up with. Short of my death, of course.

This would be a rock and roll adventure. At the very worst, an interesting road trip. See some sights, meet some people. Learn and expand. I couldn't turn this down. Having experienced a whole new world of possibilities in the last few months, I was in book promotion overdrive at this point. And signing on to this thing was the next logical step. Long had written paragraph after seductive paragraph about how he was experienced in handling the promotion of his books himself - press, public appearances, all of it. His emails betrayed a sense of affability, if not advanced levels of self-deprecation. He just seemed...*harmless*. He would refer to himself in his emails in this way:

'P.S. - I may now be an ultra-conservative, right-wing Christian wacko, but
I'm still a lot of fun! '

I had a good feeling about him. And he said he would handle all of the necessary arrangements to make it all happen. Essentially, I just needed to show up and sign books. It would be foolish to say no to this opportunity.

I was *in*.

So now it was on. In its planning, this little sojourn went through myriad changes, from its humble and innocent inception as a fun-filled trip to sunny Florida with Alison with a 'convenient appearance' thrown in, through to a full-blown five-date string of appearances across three

American states. I don't want to gloss over this part as I tell this story. I want to detail the many machinations of this trip's planning.

I have to say there was enough bluster in these emails to entice even the most skeptical *Dateline* viewer. I just wasn't sure how much of it was actually real and how much was imaginary. Everything was described with just enough bombast to make it impressive and yet still believable. Hey, the guy had done this before. He knew what he was doing. These were my conclusions. It mattered very little, as I had already made up my mind that I was committed.

All kinds of ideas were being volleyed into my inbox in August. It was weirdly exciting. The first brainstorm, on August 20, was a tour of four cities - Orlando, Atlanta, Nashville, and Jacksonville. In this permutation, a '*chicken-n-waffles-eating, Michael-Jordan look-alike travel assistant*' would be accompanying us. We would be travelling in an '*incredibly pimped-out ride*'. I liked the idea of seeing some of these cities I hadn't been to yet, but I had to ask about the travel assistant. Was this the guy that would be saying, "*Hey, does this handkerchief smell funny to you?*" just before I closed my eyes having succumbed to chloroform? I had to know about the need for a travel assistant, and so I asked. I was told that this guy was an old friend of Long's from the Florida music scene, and that he had travelled all over the country with Long as his '*compadre, personal assistant, and security guy*'. He added that he had the chops of John Bonham and that we would be immediate '*homies*'. The optimist in me smiled proudly. The realist in me furled its suspicious brow. As it often did, the optimist prevailed. Maybe a more apt characterization would be *thrill-seeker*. Or maybe *sucker*.

Nonetheless, I took the when-in-Rome approach. I'm a perennial Canadian - I see the good in everyone and everything, and I assume that these mildly unusual things are just part of some cultural sphere I simply haven't experienced yet. This little journey might even be life-enriching, if I could manage to keep that chloroform rag off of my face.

Long had a battery of ideas for this tour, and they just kept coming. It began as a joke, but he pitched me on an idea to deploy this heaven-and-hell theme for the tour, wherein he would play up his role as a Jesus receiver and I would in turn push the sex, drugs, and rock and roll thing for myself. This never did come to fruition, thankfully.

Long's big thing was always to take the road less traveled. Do things a bit differently. Get some attention. The venues he was trying to secure for us would be anything but bookstores - he wanted nightclubs, music shops, coffee houses. His theory was that people who would read our books would be more accessible in these venues than they would in a bookstore. His next idea would appeal to my vanity.

Long postulated that since his Michael Jordan-doppelganger friend played drums, he sang, and I played guitar, we should add a musical component to the proceedings. Now this thing was turning into a bloody carnival. But, as I did throughout this torrent of proposals, I worked through the pros and cons of this idea. My band had just parted ways six months previous and I missed playing. It would be fun to jam a couple of songs in a different city each night. I took a decidedly Pollyanna approach to discourage myself from acknowledging the several logistical nightmares that could have easily arisen from trying to integrate a musical performance piece, because this whole thing was Pollyanna now - it was becoming something that bordered on not being quite so real anymore. The music idea was in play for a while, but after coming to my senses I suggested we pull the plug on the concept and Long conceded.

By November, the cities starting becoming interchangeable. Knoxville was in the mix now, and Nashville was out. I was bummed about this, as Nashville had become one of my favourite places in the past couple of years. It had been the only city in the twelve year history of He-Man to be repeated back-to-back as a destination.

He-Man is the stupid frat-boy name of the guys' weekend trip I go on with my university buddies every summer. The event started back in 2001 with the intention of traveling to a different city in the US each year to see a sporting event - Cleveland to see LeBron in his first NBA season, Chicago to see Glavine get his 300th win at Wrigley Field, Penn State to see a Nittany Lions football game before the Paterno scandal (so much for wearing the Penn State hoodie I got on that trip). The attendance for He-Man typically fell somewhere between fifteen and twenty gentlemen, but as the years progressed and life increasingly got in the way, the crowd thinned to a much smaller group. Sometimes it's alternately referred to as Me-Man, because the agenda is much looser now. Somewhere around 2007 the sporting event thing got dropped in favour of focusing more on what the cities themselves had to offer - Boston, Philly, Detroit, Charlotte, and for the past two years, Nashville.

Nashville is a fun little place. A place where afternoon drinking is a time-honoured tradition. It kinda takes you by surprise the first time you experience it. Our first year in Nashville we got started around noon at Jack's BBQ on Lower Broad, and the afternoon just lasted all day. Nashville had overwhelmed us with never-ending bars showcasing master-class musicians, two serious vices for my pals and me. We left Nastyville broken men that Sunday night, but not too broken to return the following year; this made Nashville the first ever back-to-back He-Man destination. Say hello to Shawn at the Whiskey Bent for us the next time you're there. She's a hell of a singer, one of the last of the unplucked gems.

He-Man is the last annual travelling event my group of friends has managed to salvage, pared down from so many that took place years ago - golf tournaments, cottage weekends, hockey tournaments, all kinds of trips. But times change, and people change. I've always had an affinity for annual events, as I feel like they almost serve as promissory totems in life that can be enjoyed just as much by looking forward to them as actually experiencing them. I used to do a little event on my birthday every year that I called The Birthday Tour, but it fell by the wayside too. It had to - it involved building colossal meals using my favourite items from various fast food restaurants.

Every year on the day of my birthday, I would jump in the car and drive around town collecting my bounty from various drive-thrus to bring home and eat. A couple of sandwiches, maybe one or two sides, some drinks. Desserts were completely unnecessary and unwelcomed. Didn't need 'em. The Birthday Tour menu tended to vary slightly from year to year, but some items were always standard. Like Taco Bell's Fries Supreme, the nucleus of every Tour meal I had. That never changed. Usually the lineup was selected from the following items – a Big Mac from McDonald's, a Whopper with cheese from Burger King, Fries Supreme from Taco Bell, onion rings from Burger King, poutine from KFC (that's fries with cheese curds and gravy for my friends outside Canada), a root beer from A&W, and a Dr. Pepper from Taco Bell. Sometimes if I wanted to change it up, maybe a Wendy's chicken burger, a Taco Bell bean burrito with sour cream, or a McChicken might find its way onto the Tour menu. Arby's was in there too sometimes.

Of course, this event could never last. I gave up The Birthday Tour years ago. The other day Alison and I drove past a billboard displaying KFC's 'Build Your Own Bucket' option, and I laughed maniacally after shouting the phrase and inserting the word *birthday* between the words *own* and *bucket*.

"Yes!" I shouted. *"The Birthday Tour returns!"*

Alison shot me a pensive glance. "It's sad that that's what you want" she said, smiling. And as I continued my pre-birthday caterwauling, I did think about how sad that really might have been, and why.

꒰ᵒ

For a while, Long's emails stopped coming.

During this interlude, I had re-evaluated my involvement in this little caper, and I always went back to the inclusion of this third party 'security guy'. It seemed obvious that this security entity was probably just some dude that wanted to get away from whatever life situation he may have been in to rip it up a bit and pretend he was some sort of touring rock star. Security was obviously not required for this excursion, nor was any kind of personal assistance as far as I could tell. But this stuff was the impetus behind this entire venture. It was fantasy. Make believe.

But all things being equal, why wouldn't I also have a 'security guy'? A 'personal assistant'? A 'manager'? If nothing else, I might actually really need a security guy to negate the potential threat of that chloroform handkerchief. By this point I had told my friends about this little trip, and one of them indicated that he might be interested in joining in on the fun. His name was Steve Flemming, or as all of his friends and the police call him, Flem.

I had known Flem for years, we lived in the same dorm at Laurentian University at different times but had shared the same group of friends. Flem was that guy that relished an excursion like this. He was that special chap in the gang that everyone knows who, after some drinks, will do things that will both absolutely terrify you and make you laugh until you can no longer breathe. Flem comes complete with a built-in compendium of legendary tales of which he is the star, a good number of which probably should not be told in these pages.

The secret to Flemming's success in staying out of jail during his adventures lies in a charm that's both disarmingly funny and maybe a bit disturbing at the same time. I think he gets away with this stuff because people are confused by what he's doing, but also because they can't believe he's actually doing it. And because he's always laughing like a goddamn lunatic while he's at it.

So around the middle of December I was wondering what would become of this little adventure. Emails from Long had ceased. I didn't have solid confirmation that the whole thing was a go, as only a stop in Melbourne, Florida was confirmed to be booked. I began to wonder if Chris Long was just a lot of tin foil and not much heroin. I held off on booking my flights. Knoxville was to be confirmed, but wasn't yet. Macon was now confirmed for January 22nd. Other cities were coming in and out of the mix. There were lots of moving parts. I held out for 100% confirmation.

Then on December 20th, one month before this thing was scheduled to happen, an email came. It announced that Macon, Jacksonville, and Melbourne were now firm for January 22nd, 23rd, and 24th respectively, and that there would be something in Knoxville - either a bookstore or a coffee house on the 21st. The email laid out a crude agenda naming the dates, cities, venues, and players. Long's son was also now coming along to handle 'merch'.

The agenda prescribed travel times, and the suggestion that we'd be staying at people's apartments. I opted for hotels in my response to this email, worded as politely as possible. I was up for the rock and roll experience, but I drew the line there. When Long suggested sharing rooms to cut costs, I politely declined. This was the one thing I was pretty particular about. I've slept in plenty of strange and unfamiliar places in my younger life, and I did appreciate that Long was trying to spare the expense of hotels to offset my flight costs, but no thanks. Hotels it would have to be.

Based on the uncertainty, I still wasn't sure I wanted to involve Flemming in any of this. I still didn't know what this thing really looked like. Knoxville was morphing into Chattanooga now, as both venues seemed to be playing hard to get with Long based on the emails he sent me. I had no idea what to expect next. This could be a gong show of epic proportions, and if it was, I didn't necessarily want to expose Flemming to it. But, one night leading up to the Christmas break Flem and I were out for dinner in Toronto, and he invited himself along anyway. Turns out I didn't even have a choice.

"You still going on that thing in January?" Flemming asked.

"Looks like it. Some stuff still needs to be worked out, but most of it is booked."

"I could use a getaway. I'm gonna come with you. Let's get an RV and crank things up a bit," Flem suggested.

Not many things ever stood in Flem's way. He had owned a pink Cadillac at one point, and had bid for and unintentionally won the Pope's boat on eBay (extra charm was required to get out of that scrape). He was a few minor details away from buying a school bus years ago, for the purposes of eliminating logistical problems that prevented us from drinking while on route to events. Such is Flemming's outlook on life. Have a good time all the time.

Shortly after Flemming signed on, Long sent this email:

------Original Message------
From: Christopher Long
To: Brent Jensen
Sent: Friday, December 28, 2012 12:44 PM
Subject: FINAL CONFIRMATION

Okay pardner, all dates are now confirmed.
21st - Chad's Records (Chattanooga, TN)
22nd - The Hummingbird (Macon, GA)
23rd - Young, Loud and Snotty (Jacksonville, FL)
24th - Florida Discount Music (Melbourne, FL)
I DELIVER!
-Chris

This was it. The confirmed dates of our little tour, finally cemented into place. Long's emphatic all-caps commitment promising providence in this mission was all I had. I hoped, but didn't pray, that Long's promise of delivery would be legitimate.

Three
Five Hundred Feet

~

I was ambivalent when Long told me over the phone that the Michael Jordan security detail had bailed on the tour at the last minute. That just meant less potential for uncertainty and more room for Flemming. Long was acquiescent when I suggested that Flem was coming, but I sensed that he was a wee bit reticent based on a perception he may have developed after reading *No Sleep 'Til Sudbury*.

"So your buddy Steve, is he a big drinker too?" Long inquired through the slight crackle of our telephone connection. This was interesting, seeing as Long had initially wanted to exploit the sex, drugs, and rock and roll thing for dramatic effect. Now that it may have been real, I wondered if the shoe may have been on the other platform-heeled foot.

"He has his moments" I responded, stifling laughter. Flemming is a bloody monster with the booze.

"So are you guys like a Toxic Twins kinda situation, or what?" His voice took on a mildly precarious tone.

"It can get pretty Roman when Flem's around, yeah."

I had to be careful in straddling the divide between winding up Long a bit and scaring him away completely, as he may not have fully appreciated the cultural mores in play here. The social circles Flem and I moved in up here in the suburbs of Canada weren't even remotely close to being associated with harder drugs, a milieu Long had been exposed to in his earlier life enough to consider it a harbinger. Or so I gathered from his books, anyway. Long figured us for whiskey-swilling, hell-raising Hunter S. Thompson types, and I did nothing to dissuade him from this line of thinking.

We had already been through that familiar back-and-forth mutual assessment, the limit testing that is mandatory to this type of situation. We clarified our own, and each other's, positions on religion, ethical outlook, and as much in the way of personal truths that could be done within the timeframe we had. The bread was broken as far as all of the sensitive stuff was concerned. Long was that kind of guy that secretly liked to be wound up by others in a fraternal, little-brother-in-a-headlock kind of way. He expected it, and he invited it. We did well to understand each other's character.

Long called me a lot on the days leading up to the tour. Five times the day before my flight. Perhaps he figured I would develop a case of the heebie-jeebies and bail on him. But I would never do that. I could see now however, during these calls, that we would have very different approaches to this endeavour. No worries. I had already set my expectations bar nice and low to avoid any form of disappointment. I didn't expect to sell a lot of books, nor did I anticipate that people were going to line up to get an autograph from some strange dude from Canada they'd never heard of. I took a hyper-realistic tack. With Flem on board, the worst case scenario would be a boozy road trip seeing some parts of the southeastern United States I hadn't seen yet.

Knoxville was one of those places, and during one of Long's calls we discussed the fact that Knoxville was back in the mix and wanting to host a date now. It would have had to have been scheduled on Sunday the 20th and required a flight modification on my end, and after some consideration I eventually declined.

Flem and I attended a friend's birthday dinner in downtown Toronto the night before our 9am flight to Orlando, and 6am came on way fast. I don't really have a recollection of the details leading up to our landing in Orlando, but it was likely dull times anyway. I do remember Orlando weather being more than crisp enough for a jacket, which was a downer for two visiting Canadians during the month of January. I also remember finding it very peculiar that there was no chewing gum to be had anywhere in the Orlando airport. None. All kinds of candy, and yet no gum.

Anyway, now it would finally be time to meet our mysterious friend Mr. Long in the flesh. I looked down at my phone when I turned it on after we landed, and saw a couple of missed calls. Then it rang again. It was Christopher Long.

"*Word*," I answered.

"Where are you guys?" Long intoned. All business. Maybe a mild touch of George Costanza in there too. We arranged to meet at baggage claim. Long seemed hyper. Flem and I were not. We eventually made our way to him ten or so minutes later.

I knew from pictures I'd seen on the internet that Long had a penchant for the colour pink, but the hot pink beret he was wearing disarmed me nonetheless. I was ready for the painted nails, however. Long had mentioned that he had a nail 'tech'. I'm still not even sure I know what that is.

I shook his hand, daintily painted nails and all. Big smiles all around. *"How you doin', man?!"*

"Brent, Steve - nice to meet you." Long's contralto voice resonated with a Jack Nicholson cadence. In fact, it was highly reminiscent of that scene in *The Shining* where Nicholson approaches the bar in The Overlook Hotel and propositions Lloyd for a drink. Great. Now I was in a goddamn Kubrick movie.

We stood for a while and exchanged some chat, then grabbed the luggage and headed for the car rental area. As I looked through Long's glasses and into his face, I saw someone that didn't quite resemble the individual I had seen through cyberspace. This sort of thing does happen, and it's to be expected more often than not I guess. But this was a bit different. As we stood in line waiting for the vehicle, Long and I continued to covertly scrutinize each other as politely as we possibly could. We visually familiarized ourselves with each other's physical appearances, trying to reconcile these real in-person representations with the hypothetical identities previously made available to us online. Long's eyes had betrayed the presence of another person in there behind them. The online version of Christopher Long was more rugged, more like Robert Downey Jr. in my mind. This guy squinting up at me here in the airport was that jocular kid waiting to be put in a headlock. This should not at all be fascinating, and yet it still was to me somehow.

Flem had arranged for the minivan from our hotel room back in Toronto the night before. We picked up the keys and headed down to the parking lot to select the vehicle we would all be getting acquainted in over the next eight hours en route to Tennessee and back again. It was about one in the afternoon.

"We already have a vehicle?" Long questioned.

"Yep," Flem answered. "Booked it last night."

"Wow, that's great!"

"We don't fuck around, Mr. Long," I smiled.

Long grinned. *"We're rockin' like Dokken!"*

This would be a phrase that Flemming and I would become very familiar with over the next while, whether or not we wanted to be.

Before the long drive up to Tennessee, there was still the matter of picking up Long's son, Jesse. He was waiting for us with their bags. I was curious.

Jesse came as advertised. Nice polite kid. Looked like a skater. No painted nails, and no fuchsia anywhere to be seen. With the initial greeting came the awareness of that great cultural schism that exists between generations. Jesse's vibe gave me the impression this distance would be truncated in short order, however. He wasn't as immediately convivial as his dad, but he didn't have to be. He was a kid.

After all the luggage was loaded up, we piled into the minivan. I didn't take notice of the make or model of the van, or at least if I did I don't remember it now. I do, however, remember being pleasantly surprised at the fact that the minivan scene had stepped it up a bit. I was expecting a lot less from this vehicle. The captain's chairs in the second row were a nice plus. It was like having your own little command centre in the vehicle, armrests and all. The last time I had been inside a minivan was when my parents owned a Dodge Caravan back in 1983. During this time, the minivan was a brand new peculiarity of sorts - not quite an Econoline, but not a station wagon either. My parents had bought one as soon as they came out, and when we passed another one on the highway en route to Florida for summer vacation that first year of ownership, my parents and the occupants of the other minivan actually waved enthusiastically at each other. I'm not kidding. I witnessed this with my own eyes from the bench seating in the rear.

As my present-day tour mates and I accelerated away from the airport and onto the Florida 528 toll road to finally begin our travels, I sat back in my captain's chair and experienced one of those moments of clarity, as you might when you're alone. I silently contemplated the idea that my first trip in a minivan since the 80s would carry with it an acute irony. Here I was, in present age, traversing the southeastern United States peddling books about my 80s hair metal experiences and tales of silly headbanging youth. The captain's chairs may have been considered advancement since then, but we were still very much in a minivan.

∽ɔ

The mind drifts as the miles and hours go by, prying fleeting ideas apart as pacifism. Random, secret thoughts come and go easily and often, moving in all directions like intermittent cognitive molecules colliding with each other. Most are unnecessary, none are preventable.

I thought about how dumb it was when people used the word *uber* as a prefix.

I don't make a lot of promises in life other than the important ones, and yet I could make the promise that I would never use the word *uber*. I feel like people strive to fit this word into dialogue, as part of the conjuring of some image that isn't real. It's a hip, flouncy expression that's used in the same manner a teenage girl would go out of her way to show off a new pair of expensive shoes. The word *uber* is like a linguistic pair of oversized Dolce & Gabbana sunglasses.

You would never use the word *uber* in the simple conveyance of an idea, or within the confines of your own home.

"Man, I'm uber-tired. I need to hit the sheets."

"Ugh, the dog's been shedding and now the carpet's uber-hairy".

Words like *uber* share similarities with the raft of bullshit words and phrases that define modern business lingo, which is an entire lexicon of foolishness. Most of the stuff I hear isn't even immediately conceivable. Like the phrase I heard the other day - *all the way to bright.* As in, *I like that idea. Let's take it all the way to bright.* This is laughable crap, because there are so many other expressions or articulations that could be used instead. But the absolute worst example is the use of the word *vet.* As in, *make sure to provide the power point deck to Henderson so he can vet it before the meeting.* The reason why the word *vet* is so painfully dumb is because you don't *have* to say it – it's actually easier and more natural to say something else. Like *review.* Or *read.* Or *look at. Go over.*

Vet, for crissakes. Come on.

Down there in the Deep South, I got the distinct sense that not a lot of people used the words *vet* or *uber* a lot. And I was very much okay with that. *Y'all* would be music to my ears. I still did wonder about the old F-bomb though. As our new friend Mr. Long was a Christ receiver and accompanied by his not-yet-legal son, I contemplated the difficult path to be navigated during this trip. Provided, of course, I would choose to be respectful of the good book and all that stuff. Long was only just freshly minted in his new discipline though. As he reminded us back at the airport, he was no stranger to the three B's his religion so dutifully frowned upon - booze, birds, and bad language. When we were back in the Christopher email stage, I sent him an advisory to politely warn him against the presence of salty language and the brief perspectives on organized religion I outlined in *No Sleep 'Til Sudbury,* which run counter to his. He was very cool with all of it, which I appreciated and respected. And besides, he wanted to drop a few eff-bombs himself after Flemming and I eventually got going. I could tell.

We intentionally kept the cursing to a minimum around Jesse, but he was nineteen and he could hold his own. He knew what the score was. He didn't share his dad's religious affiliations, but he didn't play the rebel thing out to the hilt either. I liked that. He had a quieted sensibility that I didn't have when I was his age, and I gave him a lot of credit for it. Most kids Jesse's age would revel in the opportunities for obnoxious behaviour like the one that was currently being presented to him, and an overuse of curse words would be an essential part of the engagement. I was like that as a kid, and so were most of my friends. But as you age you realize that curse words like *fuck* can be used more discriminately, to spice language, as it were. Almost like lexical hot sauce. Expletives can provide an enhancing flavour and punctuate their element when used thoughtfully and in the right places. Overuse is unnecessary and ruinous. And typically, the folks that 'love' the hottest hot sauce beyond the boundaries of reason and to the extent of physical injury tend to be the same ones that overuse words like *fuck,* as a means to satisfy their need to be noticed, incapable of strategizing a better way to do so. It could have been a very long trip if Jesse was one of those folks. Thankfully, he was not.

As we continued north on Florida's highways, I couldn't help but notice that we seemed to pass a billboard every five hundred feet or so, and that the gross majority of these billboards seemed to carry messages focused on one of two things - eating or having sex. Ads for burger joints or diners were supplanted five hundred feet later by notices of the proximity of strip clubs or massage parlours. This cycle seemed to repeat itself over and over again. I didn't see the word *parlour* on any of the sexy time billboards, but I didn't know what else you'd call those places otherwise. Mostly just the number of the exit was named, with the promise of a 'sensual' massage. And then, five hundred feet later, I would instantly be invited to enjoy a juicy flame-broiled hamburger.

What an interesting foray into the relationship between the typical Floridian traveling consumer and the relentless marketing machine. I was surprised someone hadn't figured out how to combine these two activities to really rake in all the chips. There had to be a way. A place where one was enabled to eat and have sex at the same time seemed to be the penultimate endgame in this consumption-driven marketing orgasmatron. Maybe you could call such a place *Bangburger*. Maybe it might be called *Chew N' Screw*. There were too many lewd and lurid possibilities. Hardee's already had a leg up on the competition by working from a subliminal angle, cheeky devils. Dine in *and* eat out. As we clicked off the miles in the presence of these billboards, I wondered if Long's god was still watching over America.

Eventually all of these triggers turned my thoughts toward a capitalization on consumption as it related to books, and the three most consumed themes of the literary day - vampires, sex, and science fiction. When Pearl Jam's *Ten* was unleashed upon us in the early nineties, the floodgates burst open immediately afterwards to release legions of unrightfully copying cats. The same thing happens in every musical genre, every artistic medium, and so on, and it's been happening forever. You see a guy panning gold nuggets down the river, look out – there'll be a hundred prospectors rubbing up against him with their pans in that same water in a New York second. Things haven't changed much over the years.

In my minivan delirium I lazily wondered if it might be easier, given the initial positive response to *No Sleep 'Til Sudbury,* to try cranking out a *Fifty Shades of Twilight* next. Maybe earn a moderate living as a writer, albeit as a literary charlatan.

Another part of my mind instantly repudiated this idea. This was something I could never really be comfortable with. I hate phonies, and I hated that we were all greedy consumers. But now, America was right here in front of me; she was unfolding slowly before my bleary eyes as I navigated her. And she was ripe for the consumption. Five hundred feet at a time.

Four
CRM 114

~

Rock and roll music being the *raison d'etre* of this little excursion, it was absolutely mandatory that it be celebrated with due reverence. Poor Flemming and Jesse. They had to listen to two rock writers blather on through extended pissing contests contrasting Zeppelin albums and which band sucked less, Dokken or Poison, and why. Our conversations were varied but unfailingly musical - they spanned decades of loved and hated bands and their minutiae, personal experiences related to music, and even one or two one-upper Skunk Baxter factoids. It was glorious.

Long was good enough to bring with him an assortment of CDs for the occasion, music mostly apropos of our present circumstance. It was a fun little collection, selected with equal parts taste and sarcasm. I remember most of them:

Billion Dollar Babies – Alice Cooper
Van Halen II – Van Halen
The Southern Harmony and Musical Companion – The Black Crowes
Bebe Le Strange – Heart
Lick It Up – KISS
Rocks - Aerosmith

Leather Boyz with Electric Toyz - Pretty Boy Floyd
Breaking the Chains – Dokken

He also brought the newest New York Dolls record, which we listened to between Macon and Jacksonville. I didn't care much for it and I was mildly glad when it was over.

Every self-respecting musicphile will have a Top Five, Top Ten, maybe a Top Twenty list of favourite records that can be recited at the drop of a hat. However, they will never have just one standalone favourite. Any real music lover worth their salt will never have one absolute, be-all-end-all favourite album. Because as a true music fan, it would be impossible. Everyone knows this. And besides, it would limit the musical pissing contest proceedings drastically.

Back in university dorm, I used to use a freshman's music collection as a predictor of their personalities and what I thought they may be like as people before I got to know them. Some didn't need to be evaluated with much consideration – one year, a guy moved in and unloaded a tape collection featuring nothing but Slayer, Megadeth, Exodus, Kreator, Bathory, and a few other thrash metal bands I hadn't heard of. He ended up being thrown out of dorm before the end of that year for, among other things, trying to run a fork through the abdomen of your humble narrator. True story.

But that was an easy assessment. It was the people who had Kool Moe Dee's *How Ya Like Me Now*, Def Leppard's *Hysteria*, Garth Brooks' *No Fences*, and Madonna's *True Blue* in their collections that weren't necessarily showing all of their cards. The correlation I made in a case like this would be that these people didn't really like music at all, except as a representative social totem that ensured no waves would be made relative to their perceived social normalcy. Pure vanilla. I kept a close eye on these folks.

Every now and again I'd see a collection that intrigued me and made me want to know more about the collector. People who would bring in Paul Simon's *Graceland*, or Springsteen's *Nebraska*, in a place where Wu Tang Clan would have been regarded as being more of a statement of implied coolness. Neil Young's *Everybody Knows This Is Nowhere*. The Grateful Dead's *Anthem of the Sun*. These were collections that brought the possibility of depth and substance. Something a little less obvious. These were people I wanted to learn more about, and I was generally glad after I did. These assessments aren't sweeping generalizations, because there are loads of other personality subsets to consider, of course. But your music collection is nonetheless very telling of your personality, particularly when displayed in a public setting. Your music collection can be my window into your soul, more reliable than the Minnesota Multiphasic Personality Inventory. That's right. Validity scales and all.

ᖰᵒ

Onward we moved through America. After we had made our way through all of the initial prescribed chat, somewhere around the Florida-Georgia border, Alice Cooper's *Billion Dollar Babies* was inserted into the player. My ears perked up.

This aural circus of an album starts off appropriately with "Hello Hooray", Cooper as carnival barker shouting out the title to all those bands that would later try to replicate his macabre tongue-in-cheek absurdity but always fall short. This record was Cooper at the height of his bizarre splendour, when his greatest strength lie in his ability to evade anyone who sought to put a finger on him. No one could - he mixed well-written conventional classic rock hits and astute political sensibility with songs about dead babies and dentist's drills. The guy was untouchable. The real *gravitas* behind all of those schmaltzy tropes arose from the fact that Cooper forced you to take him seriously in his early days, much in the same way Jason Voorhees did - via that initial shock at this new, twisted malevolence that was unfolding. Alice Cooper and Jason Voorhees had this in common. Cooper's shock value ended up having a longer shelf-life than Jason's did, but somewhere around 1983 both figures began their inevitable descent – Cooper was hospitalized for severe alcoholism, and Jason was subjected to 3-D schlock and improbable sequel silliness. Super ironically, these two would join forces in 1986 to celebrate their mutual shark jump with Cooper's single that he wrote for the movie *Friday the 13th Part VI: Jason Lives* entitled "He's Back (The Man Behind The Mask)". And it all made perfect sense. In the Coop's case, he did what he had to do to survive not only on the charts, but literally *in life* as a prolific substance abuser. I understood his position, and the strength of his early-career achievements negate his misguided 80s output in retrospect. The 80s were challenging for a lot of artists who defined themselves in the 70s. Like Cooper, Jason Voorhees' biggest problem was also his ability to stay alive. But, in a converse way - his continued survival actually diminished his credibility as his movies got cheesier and cheesier.

Anyway, several years before the 80s squandered the legitimacy of once-powerful things, *Billion Dollar Babies* shocked quite legitimately and rocked undeniably. The record is mostly brilliant, and I say mostly because it always gave me the impression that Cooper ran out of quality material right around track number eight.

Billion Dollar Babies powers through equally awesome classic rock hit and deep cut gem alike, kicking off with "Hello Hooray" through "Raped and Freezin'", "Elected", and "Billion Dollar Baby". That's a sweet run. But the low fuel indicator light goes on during "Unfinished Sweet", as "No More Mr. Nice Guy" and "Generation Landslide" keep the ride moving. But then that's it. The wheels fall off with a string of clunkers - "Sick Things", "Mary Ann", and "I Love the Dead". As I listened to this album on the way to Tennessee, I tried one more time to give these three songs enough latitude so as not to mess up my overall experience of the *Billion Dollar Babies* album. I settled on the fact that I could maybe accept "Mary Ann" and "I Love the Dead". *Maybe.* But not "Sick Things". In the age of iTunes and iPods, I would delete that track on my version of the album. As potentially blasphemous as I understand that to be, and as hypocritical as it seems for someone who truly appreciates the album experience (which I most certainly do), I think I would still do it.

I made my own Guns N' Roses *Use Your Illusion* playlist following more or less the same rationale. I did this because the *Illusion* records were perfectly timed in terms of a retrospective career arc. I always thought that with the *Illusion* records, Guns followed their two best albums, *Appetite* and *Lies,* by representing the whole of the Guns N' Roses heart with a great big, fat, sloppy trough overflowing with the two things we loved most about GN'R – Axl's unique brand of vocal histrionics and Slash's pentatonic lead heroics. It was their intended *White Album,* I don't care what anyone says.

I mentioned the fact that I fashioned my own *Use Your Illusion* iPod record aloud to my rock and roll roadshow cohorts in the minivan.

"Minus the more popular songs like "Knocking on Heaven's Door" and "November Rain". Just the deep cuts, but without the filler," I added in explanation. I felt like I needed to clarify my position.

"Filler?" Long questioned.

"All the crap. "My World", "Garden of Eden", "Coma", "Dead Horse". You know."

"Did any of Izzy Stradlin's songs make it onto this blasphemous album?"

"All of 'em. Stradlin's songs are the guts of those records," I responded. I felt like this statement contained some truth.

"The unsung hero of Guns N' Roses."

"It sure as hell wasn't Dizzy Reed."

Nor bassist Duff McKagan, or so I initially thought. When I heard Duff McKagan's "So Fine" track on the *Use Your Illusion II* record, I dismissed it as aimless and devoid of any real artistry. It sounded like McKagan was trying way too hard. As a Guns fan back then, I was fixated mostly on Axl and Slash, as most fans of the band were, mostly due to the larger-than-life rock superstar images they cast down on us the same way Mick and Keef did. McKagan seemed like a soft, unnecessary cog in the Guns wheel. Messy and seemingly without any of the real legitimacy that the other original members of the band had (okay, maybe Adler too). And that first solo record of McKagan's had been a fucking monstrosity. Around this same time *The Simpsons* actually named their beer brand, the enabling elixir of the imbecilic, *Duff Beer*. I sneered at McKagan and figured he would end up like Chris Holmes. But this is where The Curious Case of Duff McKagan begins.

Before I read his book, I had come to learn in recent years that McKagan was no longer that sloppy, drunken lout that I had seen in interviews back in the glory days of Guns N' Roses. He had shed at least forty pounds, and now he was tight, lucid, and engaging. The lines in his face may have betrayed the fact that he had lived through some hard years, but he seemed like a completely different individual. A much more impressive individual.

The book validated the fact that McKagan was indeed a person who had been a rock star, not a rock star who may or may not have been a person. The gist of his tale focuses more on his return to health from unspeakable lows and his post-Guns successes, including the establishment of his own financial firm. This is an achievement that would be considered impressive for your average university grad, let alone someone who had previously been stumbling around in McKagan's outlandish shoes. For me, this story resonated much longer than the dirt on GN'R did, to the point where it was actually even inspirational – a notion that would normally be laughable considering some of the biographies that McKagan's peers have released in recent years. The aspect that sets him apart here is that he tells the story with such humility and courage that the entire idea of it is almost unbelievable. And on top of that he's actually a good writer, despite his giving much of the credit to an editor friend.

This is all utterly fascinating to me, because of the expanded spectrum that governs this story at either end of it – Duff McKagan seemed to be not just another rock and roll cretin, in my mind he was the poster boy for pathetic and unglamourous, overrated losers. But now, he's completely turned the tables on me. He looks, sounds, and conducts himself in a way I actually wish my childhood heroes would have turned out - intelligent, witty, modest, talented, and thoughtful. And he still rocks legitimately with his bands Loaded and Walking Papers. I'm actually embarrassed that I could have so grossly misjudged him, and I don't mind admitting that here. If you're reading, Duff, please accept my humble apologies. I was wrong. You've forced me to reimagine the anointments I doled out to my musical heroes as a kid.

꒰꒱

The minivan discourse continued. "Brother Louie" by Stories was on the radio. I loved this song; I always thought the Stories singer did a great job with the vocal. The one part of the performance I didn't like came towards the end of the song, during the repetition of the chorus 'Louie-Louie-Louie, Louie-Louie-Louwah', where the singer ad-libs three extra 'Louies' into the line out of nowhere, almost ruining the song in the process. You'll know what I mean if you've heard the song. It's weird. I voice my displeasure after that part plays over the van's radio.

"Whoever produced this record should have been fired for letting that goofy vocal ad-lib get into the final mix. It's terrible," I say aloud to my fellow conspirators.

"Yeah, it's bad. Almost as bad as Lou Gramm's 'seeing double-double' ad-lib at the end of Foreigner's "Double Vision"."

I laughed in agreement. That one was pretty crappy too.

"Who was the better vocal ad-libber, Axl or Mick Jagger?"

"Tough question," I say. "Are the yeah-yeah-yeah - whoo! parts at the end of "Brown Sugar" part of the lyrics, or are those ad-libbed by Jagger?"

"Not sure. It seems very structured and pre-meditated. I think it was probably just scrawled in alongside the lyrics."

"I don't think so. I think Jagger made it up in real time as the song was being recorded, right in front of the mic," I say. "Either way, as good as that is, Jagger's whoo! ad-lib after the first verse of "Bitch" is perfectly timed and nothing short of brilliant."

Years and years ago my old pal Garvey and I smoked a joint and threw on the Stones' Sticky Fingers one night, and I rewound that part at least eight times. I used to get such a charge out of it.

"I can't think of any good Rose ad-libs, except the "Knocking on Heaven's Door" one. You know – *Ay-ay-ayay-yeah*."

"I do know that one, and as big a fan as I am of Axl's, it's not one of my favourites," I respond.

"Why don't you like it?"

"Just doesn't fit. Axl's *ay-ay-ay-ay* just doesn't work within the context of that song. In "Sweet Child" though? *Absolutely*. It's one of the finest moments in that tune. But in a folksy song like "Knocking on Heaven's Door", it just seems out of place. It's too much," I reason. I'm not even a Dylan fan, really.

"There are loads of ridiculous ad-libs on the *Illusion* records. And by ridiculous I mean bad."

"Which ones?" I ask. I think about the ones that jump out at me. The *Illusion* records were Rose's grand opportunity at iconoclasm. He knew this and he made the most of it.

"That one at the beginning of "Don't Damn Me" where he makes that cartoon character noise."

"Yeah. I actually think that one's pretty clever. Your first reaction is to balk at it, but then you think, he's really reaching out to the listener here."

That's how *I* felt when I heard that, anyway. It definitely got my attention. I heard the sound in my head, but I struggled to place the cartoon character. Might have been Tom from *Tom & Jerry*. Yes, that was it. He did it to shake off the cobwebs after Jerry hit him over the head with a two-by-four.

"How about when Axl says *boy-ee* at the end of "Bad Apples"?"

"Also interesting, but I thought he was pushing it a bit with that. I always wondered what Flavor Flav thought of it," I said. "But these are all jokey examples. What about the *whoa-oh-ohhhh-oh-oh-oh* just before Slash's solo in "November Rain"? These are the special little spontaneous things that contribute that extra little bit of magic to a song. The ones you can't resist mouthing along to as you listen."

"What about Jagger's falsetto vocal intro to "Emotional Rescue"?"

"Good one, yes." I respond.

"Between that one and the "Black Sugar" vocal outro, I think Jagger beats Axl hands down."

"Nah, I don't know. What about what Axl does with alternative vocal melody when he covers other people's songs? Like when Guns used to cover "Jumpin' Jack Flash" in 1986 before they got big. Ever hear the acoustic version of that?" I ask.

"Yeah, maybe."

"Axl adds new melodies to the chorus that are all killer. Instead of just singing *it's aaaalllll riiiight nooooow*, he adds three new melody lines to the phrase that practically change the song. For the better."

"Bold statement."

"And I'm standing by it," I reply.

We had to be close to the Tennessee border now. I was momentarily stricken by the gravity of the fact that I had absolutely no idea where I was. We'd been in the van for more than five hours at this point. Twilight was forming, and I felt that smallest of tinges I always did during that time, when day concedes in its deal with the night. I'd never felt comfortable with this time of day at all, right after the sun goes down. Always disliked it. I noticed that Long's eyelids were getting heavy, and I offered to take the wheel and finish the drive. Nighttime was almost upon us.

⟡

As darkness fell, my compatriots were all fast asleep and my solitude was eminent and certain. In my weariness, I fashioned myself a post-modern Alex DeLarge from *A Clockwork Orange*, gripping the wheel with both hands at ten and two, head tilted down slightly, grinning malevolently and with purpose. The only difference between us was that I hadn't just defiled a female stranger and looted her home. And, I was driving a minivan not a sports car. My *droogies* were here though, the four of us barreling down the road under black of night. After being in the vehicle for so long I was feeling as delusional as Alex must have felt after a few drinks at the Korova Milk Bar.

I thought about a photo I had seen on the internet, which featured a latter-day Malcolm McDowell wearing the erstwhile uniform of his old 1971 *Clockwork* character Alex. This photo challenged my mind. I tried to pull ancillary meaning from it, beyond the simple irony of the image. It offered enormous possibility to people with overactive imaginations like mine. I knew that there really wasn't anything implicit behind McDowell wearing the costume now, other than a sly nod to the nostalgic. And nostalgic folks will always create purpose from these things. But I was initially more stuck on the consideration of how *A Clockwork Orange* had turned out to be a work of such pointed irony.

In its motion picture form, *A Clockwork Orange* was directed by Stanley Kubrick, a firm believer in the existence of darkness and evil in human nature. His film ends on a grim note, with anti-hero Alex ultimately returning to his violent proclivities despite having been temporarily reformed by state authorities during his imprisonment for having committed a rash of vicious crimes. The overarching message of the film adaptation seems to be that restraining the inherent evil we harbour as humans is a vain pursuit.

Originally written as a novella by Anthony Burgess in 1962, *A Clockwork Orange* included a final chapter that positioned Alex as having experienced a metanoic transformation in seeing the error of his ways. He changed profoundly after meeting up with one of his old cronies who had renounced their former lifestyle in favour of a wife, kids, and a nice picket fence life. When Burgess approached American publishers with this manuscript, he was told to drop this last chapter as it would be less appealing to an American readership. Burgess acquiesced and both the novella and Kubrick's film adaption ended the tale with Alex succumbing to his evil tendencies. Later, Burgess was said to have regretted the decision to exclude the last chapter, disappointed by the fact that the American version of the book, and especially the movie, caused people to misunderstand the true intention of the work.

Of course, the irony stems from the fact that *A Clockwork Orange*'s original intended message was an overly positive one – that people have the ability to evolve and develop into normal adults even if they were lawless teenage barbarians. The American version, however, was polarized. Kubrick's version told us that humans will always delight in defaulting to an inherent malevolence.

Beyond this irony, there was more to be considered as I drove along that dark highway somewhere in Georgia. The fact that *A Clockwork Orange* is likely more popular in its latter version is telling of our fascination with our darker selves. Television series *Dexter*'s prominence validates this fact, even if our compulsion to lead routine lives while systematically killing people as they lay detained under layers of Saran Wrap would be justified by the premise that we were doing this for some measure of good. This justification is the lining of civility that separates us from the animals. But we're still compelled by the darkness nonetheless.

As the hours crawled by in the minivan, I dwelled on these concepts and looked for any meaning, real or artificial, that could be extracted and applied to my own personal metanoia - the point I arrived at in my life where I realized that most of what I knew as a kid was invalid nonsense. I thought about the slow metamorphosis away from recklessness and disregard for responsibility into a routine life, accepting the obligations of being an adult. I also thought about the consistent temptation of regression that's always there, waiting to be accelerated by alcohol. And how easy it would be to flout authority and flip off the man. To not move forward; to not move. To just...*stay*. Peter Pan Syndrome.

At that moment I wished Alice Cooper's song "Eighteen", the paean to confused souls everywhere, was on *Billion Dollar Babies* and not his third record. I wanted to play the song to see how those lyrics about being a boy and being a man would feel as my mind received them, and whether or not they would provide any form of enlightenment to me out there somewhere on a dark and isolated American highway.

⌒つ

After my fellow conspirators awoke, we decided to stop in Atlanta for some vittles before driving on to Chattanooga and getting hotel rooms.

Something easy, like an Applebee's or a TGI Fridays. Flemming was up front in the passenger seat, forming what would be the beginning of an interesting pattern of behaviour during our group's collective time spent in the minivan. We all would take turns driving, but when Flem or I opted to drive, we moved together from back to front. Likewise for Long and Jesse. This would continue over the course of the entire trip. The divisions were unspoken but understood. Jesse drove very little, for reasons that may or may not have meant anything. If they did, I didn't need to know.

As he rode shotgun, Flem tried to find a restaurant in Atlanta close enough to the highway that we could duck into for a quick bite and continue on to Tennessee. I thought this task would have been easier based on that plethora of billboards we'd already seen announcing all manner of restaurant, but locating one somehow proved difficult now. We made some wrong turns and ended up in a section of the city that we clearly did not belong in, and needed to leave it immediately.

Eventually we found the Applebee's Flemming had sought on his GPS and thankfully avoided the possibility of re-enacting a scene from The Warriors. Everybody was pretty quiet from being in the van for so long, but more so now because we were the only white, clearly non-local people in a packed restaurant where the overall mood was reflective of the fact that the Atlanta Falcons were minutes away from being eliminated from Super Bowl contention. I thought about the week that lie ahead and how much more in touch with Bob Seger I happened to feel at this moment. And maybe David Lee Roth too.

Among the tales of life on the road in his autobiography, Diamond Dave talks about how he used to bring a bicycle along on tour and pedal around the different cities Van Halen played in the wee hours after the show, when there was no one else around. As the city slept, the educational opportunities were his for the unobstructed taking – he would ride along downtown streets, soaking up the identity of the city through its architecture. His theory in doing this was to learn about the city's character without that learning being compromised by distraction. He and the barren city were alone together, sharing a private and undistorted relationship.

Not many guys would be envious of Roth for much else outside of his command of the opposite sex, for leading a band that boasted one of the best guitar players in the history of human civilization, and maybe for the sharp witticisms he's so adept in spewing in interview situations. Yeah, my Roth envy touched on all of those points too, but I was also jealous that he had the luxury of time most of us do not, and that he used it to satisfy his urge to *explore*. Roth is a known adventurer, scaling mountains and thrashing through jungles when he's not studying to be an EMT in New York City or learning about ancient forms of everything in Tokyo.

I wouldn't call myself a *bon vivant* in the vein of someone like a David Lee Roth, but I am an explorer. Always have been. Being able to see as many American cities as possible both large and small ranks way up there for me. And being able to see them as Roth did, under the plaintive blanket of nighttime with no one else around, ranks even higher. Don't get me wrong here; some places can be defined by their people. And I do like interacting with people, quite a lot. But sometimes the organization of the religion can confound what the idea of worship is really about.

⌒๏

Back in the van and away from Atlanta, Long passed me another CD from the back seat. Heart's *Bebe Le Strange* would be our beacon to Chattanooga.

This particular Heart record isn't one of the better ones, largely because that acoustic majesty the band had demonstrated on their first two records was being eclipsed by a pressure to espouse new wave and punk with the onset of the 80s. It gets off to a strong start with title track "Bebe Le Strange", but the fourth song on *Bebe Le Strange*, "Break", is their unlistenable foray into the new wave movement. When it comes

43

on after the lovely Nancy Wilson's instrumental "Silver Wheels", I reach over to the console and depress the 'skip' button. I could never understand why later pressings of the CD contained a bonus live version of "Break". Anyway, the record's carelessness continues with "Strange Night" followed by "Raised on You", a decent tune which sounds like a Billy Joel co-write. The airy "Pilot" fills the minivan, and all is well. Songs like "Pilot" were clearly Heart's strength, and it showed later on in the 80s with *Bad Animals* and self-titled record *Heart*. "Pilot" and the next song "Sweet Darlin'" retain just enough Joni Mitchell 70s breeziness to shine through on a confused record like *Bebe Le Strange*.

I felt for bands like Heart and their 70s contemporaries when it came time to deal with the codification of their music in the 80s. Must have been tough. I pictured these bands, the Hearts, the Foreigners, the Cheap Tricks, the Styxes, the KISSes, and all the other acts of the day, stroking their collective chins and pondering their entrance into a decade that would commoditize and homogenize them. Some, like Heart, adapted and thrived. Some did not.

I wondered if people who were born in the latter part of the fifties loathed the 80s for smearing glitter and neon on their cherished musical artists of the previous decade.

They must have. I remembered recognizing the feelings of despondence and ostracism when I saw the end coming for my teenage heroes in the surge of Nirvana's musical tsunami. The 80s only had the 80s to blame for its collapse, of course. That bloat could have never lasted. The 80s created bands like Nirvana, and these bands barely touched the point of the pin to the corpulence of the 80s before it imploded all over itself.

Some of us will never be able to help but personalize these things.

Five
Not Knoxville, nor Nashville

~

I've always loved the southern United States. Robust with character and charm.

And the *accents.*

I'm convinced Southern Hospitality is a real thing. When a friend and I were in Cancun many years ago, we got to talking with a girl from North Carolina. Extremely friendly and unassuming individual. After fifteen or so minutes of chat around our cultural differences, the conversation turned to food and Southern cooking. After we had indicated a fondness for her native cuisine, she offered us an invitation to visit her in North Carolina at any time, so that we could experience it firsthand. She was willing to cook for us, two relative strangers from another country. Just like that.

I know what you're thinking. But I didn't doubt her sincerity for a second. It was evidence of the existence of Southern Hospitality. Plain and simple. She hadn't even been drinking.

The concept of Southern Hospitality is an interesting one for Canadians, who are generally known for our own benevolent approach to interacting with others. The main point of difference between the hospitable southerner and the benevolent Canadian might be that certain self-awareness that can prevent a Canadian from leaning too far forward. But I really shouldn't be throwing blankets on these things. There will always be exceptions.

"Which hotel did you guys want to stay in?" Flem was driving now, across a huge escarpment high above the rest of Tennessee.

Minutes after we crossed the Georgia-Tennessee border, Chattanooga welcomed us with a thousand shimmering lights that traced the city's dimensions in the valley below us. The view was incredible.

"Let's look for something close to the venue," Long responded.

The 'venue' was Chad's Records, a vibey little independent record store in Chattanooga. The first stop on the big tour.

I had done my homework on these places that Long had booked for us. Chad's was the one that intrigued me the most, just because of its similarities to my old teenage hangout Records on Wheels back in northern Canada. These types of places eschewed whatever culture their postal codes may have suggested they impart, Southern Hospitality included. The only culture on offer in these establishments was usually rock and roll kinship.

We drove slowly down MLK Boulevard. Chattanooga was a pretty little place, even when obscured by the night.

"Doubletree?" Flemming chimed.

"Steep" Long said. It was. I was hoping to split the difference between five-star and fleabag.

"Marriott over here," I said, pointing out my window.

We kept driving along Broad Street, eventually deciding to save some quid in getting two rooms at the Days Inn just down the road. Flem and I in one, Long and his son in another.

This hotel actually wasn't – it was a *motel*, the drive-up kind I used to stay at as a kid when my family jumped into the ol' wood-paneled Oldsmobile station wagon for a family vacation in the US of A. The only thing missing here on this night was the outdoor pool in the middle of the property. Maybe it was on the other side of the motel.

Ah, yes. The memories came flooding back. Clutching a freshly-poured Dr. Pepper Big Gulp (before DP was available in Canada), and shouting *'you don't have to be sick to see the Doctor!'* at full volume in my sister's ear. Scanning the aisles of 7-Eleven for Hostess Twinkies. Carefree times. I still remember eating my very first Twinkie, after years of having read the advertisements for them in the back pages of my favourite comics. Despite their impossibly chiseled physiques, Batman, Captain America and Iron Man all ate Twinkies regularly. *You get a big delight with every bite*, Hostess promised. And they delivered.

And the chocolate bars in the States back in those days - *man*. The wonderment I felt as I took my time to slowly peruse the racks of them, wanting to buy one of each of those beautifully elusive candy bars – PayDay, Heath, 5th Avenue, Clark, Zagnut, and on and on and on. None of these were available in Canada, and yet the States also offered most of the brands that we had up there, Big Turk among them. Big Turk was one of my favourites back in Canada, even if it did taste like it was maybe one electron away from being the solid version of insect repellent. These were fleeting concerns as a kid, if they were concerns at all. I cared even less what any of these new foreign candy bars tasted like – nougat, coconut, wafers, whatever. Didn't matter. I just wanted to devour the availability of all of them. *Consumption*. America always saw me coming, every time. She still does.

Though I still make a point of picking up a Baby Ruth whenever I visit the States, I'm more focused on the variety in American adult beverages these days. Yuengling, Blue Moon, and Rolling Rock beer aren't available north of the border. These brands would all be represented on ice in the sink of room 237 at the Days Inn Chattanooga Rivergate. Flem got PBR in cans, that predictable bastard.

"What did you get PBR for, you clown?" I asked him.

"Because you're a dick," he responded.

I threw a piece of ice at him. It missed, shattering against the painted concrete wall.

"*What did you get Rolling Rock for?*" he deliberated in exactly that same whining tone you can hear your sibling using when they mocked you in childhood. You know the one.

"It depends," I replied.

"On what?"

"On whether or not you want me to smash this Rolling Rock bottle over your head."

We laughed as we consumed our American novelties and flipped through the channels, unable to choose between *Jersey Shore* and CNN. The smouldering Erin Burnett came on CNN hosting *Out Front*. CNN it would be.

I tilted my head towards Flemming. I was glad that he had joined me on this trip. "You ever miss The Farm?" I asked. His eyes moved from the image of Burnett sitting cross-legged opposite her male guest, down to the pallid bedspread.

"I don't miss living *in* The Farm, but I miss living *at* The Farm."

I understood what he meant. The Farm was a dilapidated old bungalow that sat square in the middle of a massive swath of largely unkempt property thirty minutes north of Toronto. Four guys fresh out of Laurentian University lived there, along with a consistent entourage of maybe twenty or thirty more guys and gals, me included. It was a dump. A flophouse for drunks known and unknown, and the centre of the party universe for all of us during that time. Weekends were almost unbelievable. Unique strangers were always invited back to the property after the bars closed, because we thought it was funny. Many amusing and hilarious characters spent time at The Farm. A girl who was an opera singer came back one night, and some of the other guys tried to sing with her while Flem wore her clothes.

There were shit-talking callouts galore, resulting in some very funny capers. Kent 'Blaze' Bailey, a former high school track & field star and also a primary Farm resident, insisted one night after a few beers that he was fast enough to outrun fire. The next logical step of course, was to challenge this proclamation. Along with Flemming, the remaining two primary Farm residents, Wylie and Jammer, agreed on a logistical framework that would conclusively prove or disprove Blaze's claim. Blaze would be required to sprint a certain distance holding a jerry can filled with gasoline pouring from its spout. After a few Mississippis, the trail of gasoline would be lit at Blaze's starting point and the race would be on.

Fire won. Claim disproven.

Towards the end of the residency at The Farm, which I believe lasted just longer than two years, it was definitely time to get out. There was a running bet as to when the toilet was going to finally fall through the floor and into the basement. A couple of years after everyone bought homes of their own and moved on with their lives, I joked in the speech I gave at Blaze's wedding that the shower at The Farm was the only one I'd ever used that actually made me less clean than I was before getting in. It wasn't uncommon to draw the shower curtain and unleash more than a couple of earwigs.

That was life on The Farm for us as younger men with lesser responsibilities. I missed it sometimes. At that moment, as we sat on the bed crunching potato chips and drinking Yuengling at the Days Inn, I felt like this trip might be a week's worth of Farm-living redux. We wouldn't be able to shoot roman candles at each other within the cozy confines of our Days Inn room, but that was just as well. Still, Flemming was likely plotting a sizeable fireworks purchase now that we were seeing the roadside stands with regularity. He loves fireworks like Kanye loves himself.

My favourite characteristic of Flemming's is that he never, ever takes himself too seriously. He sees humour in absolutely everything. I've always admired the fact that he approaches life with a big, ridiculous smirk and a devil-may-care attitude. I recognized the fact that I could afford to be a bit more like him in that way. On this trip, the nexus between man and boy would prove much more murky and perplexing than usual. And with Flemming aboard, man hardly stood a chance.

Just as Flemming flipped away from Erin Burnett in favour of the Jersey Shore reprobates, there was a rapping on the window of our room. The curtains had been pushed wide open earlier, and I saw Long's bespectacled face on the other side of the window peering in. I gestured with my left hand to come in, not realizing the door automatically locked. Long tried the door. No luck. Flem and I laughed and shrugged our shoulders at the outcome, a reaction that would repeat itself over the course of the trip and yield just as much entertainment every single time. Long really was the little brother who wanted the headlock, and he was definitely getting it.

Flem got up to open the door. Long took two reticent steps inside, a bemused look on his face.

"Uh...why are you guys in your underwear?" he asked.

"Why aren't *you* in *your* underwear?" Flem retorted.

Long chose not to answer the question, opting instead for an uncomfortable snicker.

"Just checkin' in," he said. "How's the room?"

"It's no Marriott," Flem mumbled with a grin. We were all comfortable with each other now. The winding up continued.

Flem looked up at Long from the TV. "You want to come out for drinks tonight? Maybe get some food?"

"I think Jess and I are going to hang back. I have some work I need to get done."

"What kind of work?" I asked.

"Ah, you know – the blog, some deadlines. Get ready for tomorrow. That stuff."

"Okay."

I wondered if there was anything I needed to get ready for. We still had almost another twenty-four hours before the record store appearance the following night.

"Enjoy your night, gentlemen," Long intoned in that deep Nicholson brogue as he closed the door behind him.

⁓ↄ

Because midnight had already passed, finding a place to grab a bite in a restaurant other than McDonald's would require some walking. Predictably, the streets of downtown Chattanooga were quiet on a Sunday night. I looked forward to taking in some of its small town charm by daylight the next day. After some wandering around we eventually came upon a little roadhouse-type place that was still serving food, tucked back in behind the main streets.

We would be the only patrons in this place, aside from a small group of guys packed into a corner booth. They were all clearly lubricated. Each puffed up their chests and talked loudly over the others whenever the waitress came around, lending so much more credence to Desmond Morris' *The Human Animal* than any of them could realize. Eventually their quarry made her way over to us.

"Hi, my name's Shelley. What are y'all having?" our twentysomething waitress asked. The accent was prominent.

"I'll have a Yuengling, please," I responded.

"What now?"

"*Ying Ling*?" I raised my eyebrows as I enunciated, as if that would provide extra assistance in helping her to understand what I was requesting.

"We don't have that here," Shelley said in anticipation of my next ask, sensing it wouldn't be Budweiser. Maybe it should have been.

"Do you have Heineken Light?" I don't know why I asked. I knew she would respond in the negative before the words left my lips.

"No, sorry."

Flemming sneered. "You jackass, *come on!*" Human animals.

"Alright, alright. What do you have that's local?" I asked.

"How about Imperial Pilsner?"

"Done" I said. I still don't know the difference between pilsners, lagers, and ales, though I really should. Flem got a Samuel Adams, and we ordered food.

Shelley returned with our beers. "If you don't like that one, I can replace it with somethin' else if you like," she drawled as she put the bottle of pilsner in front of me.

"Thanks, Shelley."

"Y'all must be from out of town, where you here from?" the quarry asked.

"We're down here from Toronto," I responded.

I mentally glossed over some of the instances in which I had said those words, *down here from Toronto*, in the number of exchanges I'd had with various northern and southern Americans over the years.

Most knew where Toronto was, and if they had visited, they always made an effort to mention that they found it clean and friendly during their visit.

"Just on vacation?" Shelley didn't seem to care about the cleanliness or friendliness of Toronto. The easy answer to her question was *yes*.

"We're down here to promote a book he wrote," Flem said, gesturing at me.

"Really? What kind of book?" The look on her face didn't align with the intonation of her voice. She likely thought we were lying, and no longer too far removed from our friends of the same species over in the corner booth.

"It's a book about Christian Nationalism," I said with a straight face.

"Oh, okay."

I started laughing. "I'm kidding. It's a book about my experiences growing up in a small town in Canada as a music fan." After completing that sentence, I wasn't sure which description would be more interesting for Shelley.

She was a bit younger, and as we discussed the book she confessed that she hadn't even heard of most of the bands featured in it. Hearing that made me want to feel bewildered, but realistically it really just made me feel removed. Weird feeling.

"I'm gonna buy yer book online, I prefer e-books," she offered.

"I appreciate that, thank you." I meant it, even if she didn't.

Flemming and I had a few more beers and chatted with Shelley about our respective countries before settling the bill. As we talked, I wondered to myself about the appearance the next day and what it would be like, in this Chattanoogan indie record store owned by Chad.

c━ᗁ

Early the next morning, there was a knock on the door. Flemming and I both hate waking up in the dark, so we had opened up the curtains before going to sleep the night before. Standing on the other side of the window was Mr. Long, in a green jacket and a pink children's bonnet atop his head. We laid in our beds looking at him for a minute. Then I gestured for him to come in.

"Come on in," I croaked.

He immediately reached for the door, twisted the knob and pulled, but no dice. Locked. He grinned like Jack Torrance as he shook his head.

"Got me again," Jack said from the other side of the door. I was laughing too hard to feel like Shelly Duvall.

Flemming opened the door for him. He remained outside in the unseasonably chilly Chattanooga climes. In addition to his bonnet, he carried the pink Hanna Montana purse I had first seen in pictures, and then again after it had been pointed out by Jesse during a fuel stop in Georgia. I hadn't been quite sure what to make of this.

"Get in here man, it's freezing," I said.

Dude never did look like a lady, but these pink accessories challenged me to wonder...*why*. But maybe there was no need to wonder, no need to know. Didn't matter, maybe. I pushed it to the back of my mind for the moment.

"Want to go for breakfast? Have a look at the town afterwards?" Long asked.

"Absolutely."

"There's a place right beside Chad's Records called Toast," Long said.

"Perfect. You're really doing your homework, huh?"

"Like I said, man, *I deliver*."

"Well, I don't care what Poison says about you, Long. *I like ya!*" I offered in my best Nicholson, slapping him heartily on the back on my way past him to the shower.

The four of us decided to walk to breakfast. The sun was out and the fresh, crisp air was welcomed. Our room unfortunately smelled a bit like The Farm.

Chattanooga was a pleasant, peaceful little place. Kinda like Nashville's unassuming kid sister. We walked about town with heads swiveling slowly from side to side, just taking in the calm of this place. Joni Mitchell could have been describing Chattanooga when she wrote "Morning Morgantown".

"Toast is this way, gentlemen" our pink-besotted tour guide told us.

We followed Long for a few minutes before stopping to focus on the huge mural that was painted on the side of the old brick building that stood between our group and Toast. Massive red and white block letters projected the name of this evening's venue – CHAD'S RECORDS. Nice. Looked cool so far.

It was still earlier than ten in the morning, so the place was closed. I approached the front of the building to have a look inside. Before I could press my hands to the glass to block out the sunshine and get a proper look at what Chad had on offer within, I saw the promotional poster Long had created for us that featured the covers of our books alongside our smug faces. It was taped to the inside of one of the huge panes of glass that made up most of the storefront. TONIGHT!!! LIVE IN PERSON AT CHAD'S!!! had been added by someone (likely Chad) in handwritten Sharpie at the bottom of the poster.

I felt a mix of apprehension and pride as I looked back at my digitally rendered self through the window. My reaction to situations like this one was one of optimistic caution. It's always been my way to anticipate the worst. It's a defence mechanism I had carried around with me since my disquieted youth. It wasn't that I was unsure of myself now. I wasn't. Just apprehensive.

This all began at a young age. Likely before I was even eight years old. I was around that age when my grade three teacher selected my speech to represent both grade three classes in our elementary school.

The way this worked was, every kid in every grade starting in grade three through to grade eight had to write a speech, and deliver it to the rest of their class. One representative was selected for each grade to give their speech in front of the entire school, from the stage in the school gymnasium. Fairly serious business for an eight year old kid. My teacher selected me to represent grade three, and I was thrilled. The night before the event I wrote out my speech, about Canada, in big capital letters so I could read it clearly during my presentation in front of all my fellow students. The next day, I sat and watched from one of the six public speakers' chairs lined up against the wall nearest the stage, as the teachers led their classes into the gymnasium one by one, filling the gym up completely. I was stoked, and I was prepared. And I was also first. Just before my name was called, I reached into my pocket and pulled out my speech, unfolding it in preparation to proudly deliver.

Tammy sat beside me, representing grade four. Pretty, confident, and with her chestnut tresses curled into the best Farrah Fawcett her mother could muster, she whispered to me.

"You were supposed to memorize your speech."

What? What was she talking about?

"We all had to memorize our speeches. You're not supposed to read," Tammy repeated. I looked down the aisle of public speakers. No papers. Every one of them had memorized their words.

I was just about to get up. An invisible leaden weight held me down on my chair. I was frozen. Humiliation. Fear. My teacher had neglected to tell me I had to memorize my speech.

My name was called from the stage.

"Just try not to rustle the paper too much," Tammy said, which I took as sincere advice. I'll never forget those words as long as I live. Traumatic public speaking experience number one.

Right up until my university days following that experience, I was terrified of public speaking exercises of any type. Of course, as wily and determined as I was at university in avoiding any situation in which I would have to speak publicly to a large group, even dropping classes sometimes just to alleviate the panic of the prospect, I was bound to find myself in at least one or two situations where getting my degree was contingent upon giving a presentation. It would be inevitable.

In one of my second year psych classes, I would have to give a fifteen minute dissertation on a topic I don't remember now. I was terrified at the notion of this, and it was always in the back of my mind every day leading up to the scheduled date of the engagement. I was living in dorm then, and ridiculous things went through my mind constantly during those years. A period of magical thinking and gross irresponsibility. For this speaking obligation, I figured that maybe if I self-medicated a bit, it would take the edge off and I could relax somewhat as I gave my presentation. Magical thinking indeed.

About ninety minutes before the class, I dropped by the room of one of the guys in dorm who had a steady supply of dope, and I related my conundrum. He cackled as he rolled up a massive joint. This should have been the first indication that this would be a poor idea. I smoked most of it by myself just out of pure anxiety, not a wise decision for someone who barely smoked recreationally at that time. Very, very poor ideas these were. But I was wracked with nervousness. During an age when I made some of the poorest decisions of my life, this one would prove to be up there with some of the worst.

As normal, I walked down the path to the classroom building. What wasn't normal was how buzzed I was. I had a handle on it leading up to class time, but when it came time to stand up in front of the class for my presentation, things got weird. Reading wasn't an issue this time, as it wasn't a public speaking exercise *per se* – it was the presentation of the results of some project initiative. So everyone read from their notes, albeit some a bit more timidly than others. As I started to read, my mind began to invent all of these ridiculous scenarios, all unfolding simultaneously. None of these ideas had anything to do with the presentation material – they were bizarre considerations, using the same ideological framework that dreams do. Reality and logic played very minor roles.

As I realized this was happening, in front of everyone, my pulse quickened and my heart started to pound like it was trying to escape from my torso. I wondered if it might detach itself from its ventricles, and if I would collapse right there. I was panicking, but trying to keep it together. All of these crazy thoughts were careening around my brain. My discomfort was compounded by the intense paranoia that everyone in the class knew what was going on in my mind, and that I had smoked that huge joint before class. I felt like they knew somehow. I started sweating. I continued to read, as I was determined to get through this nightmare. I felt beads of sweat trickling down the sides of my face, and that made it even worse. What were these people thinking? I felt like I was starting to melt, and that made me even more self-conscious. It was a vicious circle right up until my last word was uttered. Traumatic public speaking experience number two.

Traumatic experience number three also occurred at university, two years later in my final year of undergrad study. I was writing my thesis to earn an honours bachelor degree in psychology, and doing this also required a presentation and subsequent defense of the content of the thesis at the end of the school year. Students had fifteen minutes to present their thesis, and the remaining fifteen minutes would be spent defending our findings against intentionally tough questions from the four professors who were responsible for mentoring the students throughout the year. Other professors from the psych department also attended and asked questions, as did alumni, fellow students and any-one else who may have been interested. It would be a very big crowd of people who all knew their stuff.

I decided, after having elected to forego the narcotics angle in bat-tling my stage fright this time around, that I would turn the tables on my public speaking disposition by doing everything I possibly could to excel in this opportunity. I took extra time to understand the content backward and forward. I prepared for the speaking engagement by rehearsing it over and over again in my dorm room. I anticipated every possible question. I researched thesis defences from previous years. The outcome would be different this time.

The professor to whom my thesis group was assigned was a cel-ebrated neuroscientific wizard who is regularly namechecked in UFO documentaries that appear on The Discovery Channel. Extraordinarily bright individual. While under his tutelage, I wondered many times if he was perhaps an alien himself, he seemed that intelligent. He sepa-rated the wheat from the chaff in my class right from the get-go, as he didn't have a lot of time for intellectual scallywags like me who weren't one thousand percent serious about getting into grad school to follow in his footsteps. But - there were times, where if you caught him in the right mood, he would crack the odd joke and ease up on the megalomania somewhat. These instances were extremely rare, but they did occur.

One night in the lab he and I were evaluating some of my thesis data, and his interpretation ran counter to mine. As we went back and forth about it he blurted out, *"I'm willing to wager you a large cheese and sausage pie that I'm right"*. We continued to joke around a bit more, and I was taken aback enough by his unusually liberal behaviour that it stuck in my mind, right up until the next time I interacted with him – during my dissertation.

The room was packed with students on this day, loads of professors and alumni. It was my turn to present. And I was ready this time. I could talk about my thesis for hours. In the introductory segment of the dissertation, it was considered proper etiquette to acknowledge your professors and fellow students. Because I was feeling so confident and positive, I thought I would lighten up the proceedings by injecting a small personal touch into my acknowledgement of the good doctor with whom I'd had the pizza wager when it was his turn to be introduced:

"...and of course Dr. (I won't mention his name here)*, with whom I had a large cheese and sausage pizza bet on my data interpretation."*

The crowd leaned in to gauge his reaction. He was like a god in this place. A god most of us feared. I looked over at him, then at the crowd. Then back to him. Silence. He typically emoted as though he was an android, so any reaction beyond that would be entertaining. Just not for me, as it turned out.

He scowled, squinting and pursing his lips. The words *"get on with it, please"* slowly and very coldly hissed out of his mouth.

The crowd grumbled. Some people snickered. I was deflated. I hadn't even started my bloody dissertation yet. The next thirty minutes felt like thirty hellish years. At the end of it all I still pulled off a B in the class, despite Dr. Dickhead.

In retrospect I like to think that these experiences, as wretched as they were, carry an intrinsic value. I enjoy speaking publicly now, and do so regularly. I like the general concept of interacting with people at book signings, regardless of the crowd size (or the number of weirdoes that may be involved). But that apprehension, as negligible as it may be, will always be there.

Down here, these interactions would be slightly new territory for me. I was a stranger in a strange land. If there would be apprehension, it would stem from the fact that there was no safety net here, and anything could happen.

I stared at the headshot of myself on the poster inside Chad's Records in Chattanooga, Tennessee, and smiled quietly to myself.

Anything could happen.

Six

Smashville Predator

~

"I think Jesse has a little something for our waitress," Long murmured lightheartedly as his eyes followed her back to the kitchen at Toast. The morning sun poured through the restaurant's windows like liquid gold, a high tide that raised all of our ships.

"What does Iggy Pop mean when he says *'of course I've had it in the ear before'* in "Lust for Life"?" I asked.

"My first guess is sexual connotation."

"Does it have anything to do with Vincent Van Gogh cutting off his ear and giving it to a prostitute?"

"I doubt it. But who knows with Iggy Pop? Wasn't there a movie called *Lust for Life* starring Michael Douglas as Vincent Van Gogh?"

"Kirk Douglas," I said.

Toast didn't operate under the standard dining service practices. It felt more like a cafeteria, where you ordered and paid at the counter and then poured your own coffee off to the side of the place, in front of the entrance to the bathrooms. The motif catered to a hippie metropolitan vibe, with unusual wall hangings and weird artifacts serving as the decor. It was one of those spots that demonstrated its emphasis on coffee through an artistic representation, seemingly in direct contrast with its natural surroundings in unassuming little ol' Chattanooga. Maybe I'm just old-fashioned, but it felt like an identity crisis was afoot.

Plates *clik-clunked* onto the table as our bohemian breakfasts were deposited in front of each of us. The thick vapor of steam rising from mine signaled to me that I wouldn't be eating for a while.

"The phrase *I've had it in the ear* is a popular saying in the Midwest, meaning if you've had it in the ear you've been screwed over."

"Ah. I guess that makes sense. But isn't getting screwed over usually verbally represented by having it in another orifice?"

"Well, let's see – do you think Iggy would have been more comfortable singing, *of course I've had it in the ass before?*"

"Touché," I answered.

Long smiled. "I'm worth a million in prizes," he said to Flem. Flem didn't seem to care much. Not an Iggy fan.

As we all ate and chatted, I became more keyed in to Long's pride in his son. He had invited Jesse on this trip for what would be their last period of extended time together before Jesse left for school later in the year. Jesse was living with his mom now, and while I was not at all privy to their pasts, I could see that Long was making an effort to reach out to his son and instill a more lasting connection. I silently lamented that tragic and unfortunate schism that can exist in situations like this one.

We continued to crisscross the downtown streets of Chattanooga after leaving Toast, taking pictures to serve as visual supplements to the descriptions of our travels we would provide to those who waited for us back home. I thought back to my old Kodak Instamatic, the first camera I had ever owned as a kid. Proudly, I might add.

"Remember when you only had twenty-four exposures on a roll of film?"

"And you had to be careful to spread them out over the entire vacation, and not just shoot them all off on one or two subjects?"

I was taking pictures of everything like a madman with my iPhone. Disposable images in an age of disposability.

"I like that the photo developing guy doesn't have access to things I'm taking pictures of now."

"That sounds slightly incriminating," I responded.

I knew the guy who used to work at the only photo developing shop in my hometown. I'm certain that dastardly mofo had albums upon albums of reprints he created of people's pictures he decided he should keep for his own purposes.

After a few hours of digitally chronicling everything we deemed necessary, we made our way back to the Days Inn. There was time to kill before the night's event. Flemming and I retreated to our lair and engaged our laptops. When I was finished with that I opened a Samuel Adams, inserted earbuds and scrolled through my iPod for something that would complement my current headspace.

Kurt Vile's *Smoke Ring For My Halo*.

My ravings about this record are barely tolerated by Alison, who generally supports most of the music I listen to. She particularly loathes Kurt Vile, saying his vocal delivery is monotone and annoying and his lyrics are stupid. And at first blush, Vile's lyrics and vocal delivery of those lyrics do seem like careless blather. But it's likely that I like Kurt Vile as much as I do at this point in my life for this express reason – Kurt Vile represents the low-profile underachiever. The breezy easiness he exudes in songs like "Baby's Arms" and "Jesus Fever" balances my life as a rat-racing nine-to-fiver. Vile's blasé attitude is important to me. Earlier in my life when *I* was breezy and underachieving, I had always been looking upward and aspiring towards something else. Now, Vile's music is the seditious yin to my adult working life's yang. It's entirely possible that I'm subconsciously aspiring to be more stupid at this point in my life after having gone in a different direction for so long.

This observation became more complicated recently. While watching one of Kurt Vile's videos online a few months ago, I noticed in one of them that his guitar player was wearing a Randy Rhoads t-shirt. This immediately made me feel uncomfortable. I likened this feeling to that of George Costanza when his personal and relationship worlds threatened to collide during the *Seinfeld* "Pool Guy" episode. Costanza's 'Worlds Collide' theory basically held that if his relationship world and independent world collided, they would destroy each other. They had to be kept separate in order to survive and prosper. This was how I felt about my love of Randy Rhoads' guitar playing with Ozzy Osbourne on Ozzy's first two post-Black Sabbath records, and my interest in Kurt Vile's music – the two cannot intersect or be associated with each other in any way, lest they diminish the power of what each represent in my mind. Selfish dogma, yes, but these two varieties of musical food cannot touch on my plate if they're to retain their essential meaning.

After *Smoke Ring For My Halo* faded into the ether, I searched out something that would be in keeping with the lazy pellucidity of Kurt Vile. And there it was. The Stones' impure and guileless *Sticky Fingers*. I skipped album opener "Brown Sugar" in favour of second track "Sway" and closed my eyes. I love this record.

The haphazardly crashing staccato chords that introduce "Sway" underscore the raw and beautiful genius of *Sticky Fingers*. "Sway" is deliberately indolent, and while there shouldn't really be anything special about the song, there is. Its specialness lies in the fact that the intention is for this song, and most of this album for that matter, to be anything but special. It's anti-art, even despite a Warholian presence during this period. This is music that doesn't sound organic on purpose.

The sloppy vocal harmonies and raw production embrace the 'dirty Beatles' branding the Stones had touted since their earliest days. Mick Taylor's outro guitar solo in "Sway" contains ninety-seven percent of Ace Frehley's entire lick vocabulary. The melodies of "Wild Horses" could have been done with a string section, but Glyn Johns and the Stones had the good sense to know that the spare, jangly acoustic guitar carried more legitimacy. There's so much occupancy and glorious wide open space available inside "Can't You Hear Me Knocking" that it feels like I can actually physically insert myself into it. "Dead Flowers" has had the luxury of time to blossom – when it was first released, the idea of the Stones doing country probably seemed jarring (*see also Let It Bleed*'s "Country Honk"), but it's a meaningful and even epochal part of the Stones mosaic now. "Moonlight Mile" glimpses the other side of that swashbuckling Stones swagger - the side that wrestled with drugs and unlikely emotional pain. It's the best song on this album, and it epitomizes the validation of the deep cuts argument that the really good stuff is buried deeper inside the record.

I drifted off into sleep before "Moonlight Mile" concluded.

⁓○

I'm always aware of what time of day it is, even when I try not to be. Not necessarily the precise hour, but the portion of the day I'm in – early or late morning, early or late afternoon, early evening and the nighttime. Whether I like it or not, I'm overly intuitive of that silent metamorphosis that occurs when late takes the place of early in each of these critical phases of the day. All of those times when the present is lost and supplanted by replacement. The morning only lasted all day when we were too young to recognize that it never, ever could have. Early afternoon had conceded now in Chattanooga, and it would be time to replace the taste of tin with that of glass somewhere along East Main.

Not too long into the walk, Flem and I found a big, bright place that featured way too many microbrews and a nice selection of wood-fired pizzas. Josh was our server. I put Josh at maybe nineteen, twenty tops. Great kid, instantly likeable. He had that genuinely amiable, good-natured disposition that every father wishes their daughter's boyfriend did. As Flem and I conspired the night's post-appearance events, we asked Josh for some guidance.

"Y'all might want to try some of the places up on Market Street," Josh advised after we described our interests. Over the course of our discussion with him, Josh shared that it was his first shift at this bar, and that we were his very first table. He had never waited tables before. After we had finished the pizza we shared, Flem and I dispensed with the pints Josh had recommended to us as newcomers to the area. You couldn't not like this kid.

"Let's pay it forward," Flem said as he reached for his wallet. He removed two twenties from it and dropped them on the bill. "Get Josh off to a good start with his new job."

"I like it," I responded and matched his twenties in the check holder, then folded it closed. The bill was $31.

"Thank you very much, guys. It was real nice meeting y'all," Josh smiled as he walked away. We pushed in our chairs and left.

As we waved to him from the other side of the window, Josh gestured to us with a look of concern and mild panic. His right hand went up, waving to request that we stop. We continued walking and nodded, giving the thumbs-up sign. He responded in kind with big eyes and a bigger smile. His mouth formed the words *thank you* through the window to us as we walked away.

Flem smiled as he looked up at the traffic light. Green.

"Good kid."

⌒♉

Long was waiting for us back at the hotel. T-minus ninety minutes to showtime at Chad's Records.

"Come on in," I mouthed to him and wagged a finger towards myself from inside the room after he appeared at the window. He reached for the doorknob and tried it. This never, ever got old.

I opened the door. "You guys ready?" Long asked.

"How long a drive is it?" I answered his question with my own.

"Probably about ten minutes" Long responded. I looked at my watch. It was just before six.

"Want to leave at say, six forty-five?" Another question.

"Nah, we should get there a bit earlier to make sure we have the time to set everything up, check out the venue, shake hands, you know – all that stuff."

Long loved *all that stuff*. He was a showman, a born performer. The David Lee Roth to my Edward Van Halen. Dude was a conjurer. But I wasn't complaining. He had put a lot of effort into this entire thing.

"Okay. Six-thirty good?"

"Yeah, six-thirty is real good." Long nodded with that Nicholson twang. "At six-thirty we're rockin' like Dokken."

"Pal, listen. I'm sorry, but I'm afraid Dokken doesn't rock" I noted.

He pursed his lips into that same smile I had seen in his band promo pictures as he started toward the door.

"See you guys at six-thirty."

⚬⟋⟍

We pulled into the parking lot of Chad's Records as dusk fell. It was empty.

Jesse and Flemming helped us bring our contraband into the cluttered little shop. No tables had been set up yet.

And no Chad.

The guy at the counter assured Long that Chad would be along shortly, that he was out picking something up. We waited. I ambled around, surveying this atmosphere. Flem had brought along a quality camera, and he was taking random photos inside and outside the store.

I wasn't sure what to make of the fact that no one at Chad's seemed ready to host this event. It wasn't like we were Keats and Shelley coming in to sign books or anything, but it was a bit unusual.

Just after seven, Chad showed up and apologized for the disorganization. He presented as I imagined he would – younger, thin, with brown hair that flowed down past the collar of his baggy sweater. He carried himself with a distinct bohemian mellowness. The shop was as independent as it gets, literally a leased space housing thousands of vinyl records of all sorts. Chad knew a thing or two about music.

As I asked questions about the shop, I learned from Chad that selling records in his shop was a struggle. Business was bleak, but he had owned the shop since he was a kid, back in the pre-Napster days when product flew off the shelves. This record shop was all he had ever known in life. But records weren't selling anymore.

As people showed up, Long and I signed books and chatted. Flem continued to take pictures from the back of the store. He came to the front and pulled me aside. He was laughing.

"Hey, check this out" he said, holding up the camera so that I could see the display screen on the back of it. On the screen was a shot of one of the customers who had just bought a copy of *No Sleep 'Til Sudbury*. He was holding the book up in front of his face, one eye peering back at the camera from behind the top of the book. Flem advanced to the next shot. There he was again, with his hand in front of his face. And again in the next one, turning away from the camera. For some reason this guy didn't want his picture taken. Flem had been making a game of it.

"What do you think he's hiding his face for?" Flem giggled.

"I don't know, and I don't want to know" I responded. Kinda weird. That guy had told me when I signed his book that he was from out of town, didn't live in the area. We never did find out why he hid his face from the camera that night. That was probably for the best.

At nine sharp we packed up, thanked Chad for his hospitality, and headed back to the hotel. It had been a less than conventional engagement, leading me to believe that the rest of the upcoming dates would likely be the same. No worries. My expectations bar remained in its low setting. And we always had the booze to fall back on. Flem and I had a few beers in our room before taking Josh up on his Chattanooga nightlife recommendations.

In the first establishment he suggested, the crowd seemed pretty engaging. Once inside, we chatted up some of the revelers as bleary AC/DC and Motley Crue anthems vibrated the floorboards, sticky with spilled booze that challenged the bottoms of my shoes as I walked to the restroom. On my way back to where Flem stood, I could see a group of about six women maybe twenty feet away from him on the other side of the room. They formed a crude circle and stood out because they were all dressed similarly, each wearing a cowboy hat. All appeared blasted. As I got closer to Flem I saw one of them, short and squat, break out of the circle in a sprint in his direction. About ten strides later she crashed square into Flemming's back, causing him to fall forward and toss his whiskey and Coke right onto the blouses of the two women that stood directly in front of him. With that, the stout little rhino gathered herself and wobbled back to the herd.

Flem stood there with his empty glass, palms turned upward and face wearing a "WTF?" expression. I almost fell to the floor myself, I was laughing so hard. The blouses were *pissed*. Who was this rhino woman, and what had she done that for? We walked over to the group to find out.

"Sorry y'all, she's just really drunk," a larger, taller woman stepped forward and declared. This woman seemed to be the den mother of this little group. "She's just having fun. We're here from Nashville." We stood watching as she charged someone else from across the bar, bodychecking a complete stranger but without the same (hilarious) drink-spilling results. She was in that specific alcoholic fugue where reasoning was out of the question, and likely maybe twenty minutes away from evacuating the contents of her stomach onto the floor. I didn't want to be around for that.

"Where y'all from?" slurred one of the other members of the drunken cowgirl club. I looked into her face. She instantly reminded me of Bret Michaels – same lips, same features; same heavy colorful makeup Michaels wore in Poison's salad days. Her face was framed by long wavy auburn locks that fell down from under the cowboy hat. Hair colour notwithstanding, she was a dead ringer for Michaels. Who is *male*. I may have been making this more involved than it had to be.

"Toronto" I responded to her. Her drooping eyes lifted somewhat.

"Yeah? What are you doing here?" The tone was a bit surly.

"Seeing the sights," I said.

"Well, what do you think of the sights so far?" Sassy, inebriated smile. Her exaggerated gestures flowed in slow motion.

Trouble may or may not have been brewing. I looked over the Nashville Predator's shoulder to see Flemming mending fences with the Rhinoceros. He was thick as thieves with her and the rest of the gang now.

"I'm going outside," purred the Predator. My guess was to vomit. She was wrecked. I watched her shuffle away as I walked over to join Flemming and his new friends. The leader of this group, their Captain, was still giving off a distinct maternal vibe while her intoxicated friends carried on.

We got to talking about Nashville, and how Lower Broad is for tourists in the same way that The Strip is in Las Vegas. The really good stuff is hidden away behind the bells and whistles of both locales. You could say that about a lot of cities, I guess. The real question about Nashville in my mind was, in a town so rife with thousands of varieties of quality whiskies and bourbons, why was moonshine necessary? The last time I was in Nashville, I had spied a clear glass bottle ominously marked with three black Xs behind the bar we were in. I asked the bartender what it was.

"That's *shine*, hon. Wanna try?"

I really didn't want to. But, when in Rome...

"I don't see why not," I replied.

She poured half a shot and slid it across the bar. Down it went.

Argh. So aggressive.

"Whaddya think?" the bartender smiled brightly, as if her smile would cut the depravity of the gasoline I had just swallowed.

"I think I'll pass on the full-size serving," I responded.

I shared this story with my drunken new Nashville friends and posed the question about the necessity of shine.

"That was tourist shine!" The Captain chortled. "Real shine's way better."

I didn't believe her.

"Shine is vile no matter where it's from," I lamented out loud and ordered a bourbon.

Our group began to splinter off in different directions in that familiar way that alcohol never fails to perpetuate. Flemming and I left and wandered across the street into another bar, where we happened upon some folks partaking in some sort of artistic endeavour. By the time we discovered what their objective was, it was too late to walk away. The bartender with the microphone made sure of that.

After she handed out an assortment of crayons, the barkeep instructed us to illustrate the penis of the guy standing to our immediate right. We were to draw it on the bar, which was covered in white paper. Flem was standing on my left. He would be drawing me. Great. I looked to my right, into the bloodshot eyes of a gentleman who may well have been a member of Linkin Park. Without words, his facial expression relayed the unspoken message that it was cool under the circumstances. All good to sketch out a picture of this stranger's dick in a public setting. Right then.

I figured I'd have some fun with it and draw this outlandishly massive wang that disappeared over the edge of the bar. Great big scrotum, too. Hey, the guy was there with his girlfriend, so why not? She was laughing like hell. Not sure if that was good or bad.

Time was up. "Drop your crayons!" the bartender shrieked.

She picked up a crayon and assumed the role of judge, starting at the far end of the bar and working her way down, verbally carving up either the artistic effort or the implication that the subject wasn't exactly packing.

She looked down at my drawing. Her eyes got big, and her mouth formed a circle. "Wow!" She looked up at the girlfriend. "Congratulations, honey!"

I looked over at Flemming's rendering. Ah, Flem. He had drawn a gigantic vagina. Splendid.

The bartender looked at Flem's work and reared her head back with laughter. "Winner, right here!"

On to the next whiskey bar.

⌒⊙

As I stood with my foot resting on the rail that ran the length of the bar in the next establishment we visited, I surveyed the musical talent currently on the stage. She was up there alone, with just a black Takamine acoustic guitar, singing into the PA with a voice that gleamed like justice. The lights shining behind her hair lent it a blue-black intensity that likened her to Tom Keifer at the height of Cinderella's glam-rock androgyny. The place was packed, all of these people clearly here to listen to this girl sing.

She was beyond good. She did some Ryan Adams, some Melissa Etheridge. She sang "What's Up?" by 4 Non Blondes. Nailed all of it with ease. I tried to remember the last time I had heard somebody this talented play covers in this type of setting. When the familiar chords of The Black Crowes' "She Talks To Angels" washed over the crowd, I was weakened. My surroundings fell away, and the background din of the bar was silenced. I couldn't have been more dialed in to this performance. I felt like it might make my heart burst at this moment, if only just to quantify the emotional stimulation I was experiencing. This was everything that I enjoyed about music – raw, legitimate expression, soulfulness, and stripped-down veracity. All delivered with massive skill and magnetism. Magical stuff. When it was over, much too soon, I took a few moments to languish in its remnants and consider its power.

Her set was finished, but I dared not try to engage her in conversation. The swirly portion of my evening had begun, that part where everything slows down a bit compliments of the drink. There would be no way to find the words I would have preferred to offer in appreciation of such a performance.

She walked by and looked at me as she passed.

"Really great job," I said. "Loved the Crowes tune."

"*Awwww, thank you!*" she beamed, seemingly genuinely appreciative. I nodded, and she continued on to the sound board behind me at the back of the room. It occurred to me that I may have met her somewhere before. Likely in a bar back in Smashville.

I wondered where Flemming may have been. Couldn't see him anywhere. When I turned to my left, however, I did see a familiar face directly in front of mine.

"Ah, you again" I said. It was The Nashville Predator.

"Yes, *me again*." She sounded so cross. I didn't really understand what her deal was. It was like she was trying to intimidate me for some unknown reason.

"What can I do for you?" I asked.

"Where's your friend?" she blurted.

"It's rude to answer a question with a question, you know."

She was maybe one drink away from completely emulating drunk Homer Simpson, in that early *Simpsons* episode where he says to Bart, *"I don't owe you twenty dollars, you big baloney."*

"C'mere, I'll buy you guys a shot," she propositioned. *"Where's your friend?"* Her voice got louder.

Jeez. I almost felt that she may have done away with Flemming and that this was some weird drunken attempt at a cover-up of the crime. This bird was quite strange. Glenn Close to my Michael Douglas except for the whole *attraction* bit. The *fatal* part was definitely there. The booze bolstered my nerve, though. I was impervious to any psychotic episode she may have had up her kooky sleeve. Reality was alternative now, and I was actually interested in what she might do next. There was blood in the water. I did like these situations under the circumstances.

Flem appeared, with no visible rope burns or knife wounds. I watch way too much *Dateline*.

"Hey!" he shouted.

"Ah! There you are. Let's go!" the Predator trumpeted.

We stepped up to the bar, and she ordered three Jager Bombs. Like any of us needed them. Down they went, and Predator fumbled through her purse with useless hands. She was really far gone. Just before Flemming and I produced our wallets to square up, she dramatically shoved a credit card in our faces.

"No!" Predator exclaimed. *"I got it."*

She gave the bartender the card. He returned with it a short while after, without a piece of paper to sign. "Declined," he deadpanned.

"What?" Predator spat. More fumbling. I slid my credit card across the bar to the bartender.

She stood there for a little while dumbfounded, as if not certain what to do next.

Then she looked up at us.

"Hey – I wonder if I can pay with these!" The Nashville Predator stammered. She grabbed at her tank top and whipped it up, proudly exposing her breasts. She was not wearing a bra. Flemming spit the contents of his mouth on the floor and started howling with laughter.

I actually was not expecting this, and yet I wasn't surprised. A burly doorman came over and carted her off, out into the street. The bartender returned with my credit card, and thankfully also with the slip that required my autograph. I signed off and we went outside to make sure that the enthusiast was okay. Maybe throw her in a cab. Hold her hair. Something.

She was crumpled up on the curb, eyes moist with tears. *"Get the fuck away from me!"* she shouted.

Whoa. Here comes the episode.

"C'mon, let's get you home. We'll get you a cab," Flem said.

"Leave me the fuck alone. Do you think you're better than me? Do you think you can fucking *laugh* at me?" she yelled.

The Predator was about to go completely nuclear. Her eyes were seething and she was making very intense faces.

"Hey, take it easy," I said. "We're fine, we're all fine. We just want to make sure you get home safe."

"Why, so you guys can both *rape me?*" she retorted, a little too loudly for my liking. Drunk or not, this girl was a kook.

I stood up and looked at Flem. "I'm out," I said. He shrugged.

With that, she stood up and stumbled away down the street, fading out of sight and into the darkness. We went back into the bar.

After last call was served, we decided to go back to the hotel. Instead of taking a cab, we'd walk it off a bit. A blond, larger woman wearing a cowboy hat was walking towards us on the sidewalk on our side of the street. I squinted to focus on her face. It seemed like she was moving too fast for my eyes to catch up.

I felt like I recognized her. Yes. The Captain! The ringleader of that little gang of wasted breast-flashing troublemakers from Nashville.

"Hey," I slurred in her direction. *"Where's the rest of your fucking gang?"*

She slowed down and looked at me with bemused lemon mouth.

"I'm sorry?" she intoned.

Dammit. It wasn't her.

"Oh man, I'm so sorry," I lamented. "I thought you were someone else."

Swirly.

"That's okay," she said with a weak smile and continued on.

"Time to go home, Flemming," I warbled.

Flem was bent over cackling like a bloody madman, eyes tearing up and face red with laughter. "Oh, man! I think I just pissed myself."

Seven

Macaan

~

Before our pirate ship began its lengthy slog from city to city each day the system was always the same, from Tennessee right on through to Florida. Drive from the hotel to the nearest gas station to fuel up, at the same time picking up the contents necessary for the day that lie ahead. Whatever you were having for breakfast would be picked up either at the gas station or at a Dunkin' Donuts if there was one in close proximity. One large bottle of water, one large bottle of Gatorade, and beer for that night to top up whatever was left over from last night, if anything. When we got to the hotel, the ice machine was located right away and teeth were brushed immediately (unless you wanted to brush during your pre-evening shower later), because the sink would be filled with ice in order to serve as our beer chiller in the absence of a refrigerator. Take a cold one out, load in a warm replacement. And Flem and I were becoming adept in the ways of opening non-twist off beer bottles. We moved beyond the strike plate of the bathroom door to wedding rings, belt buckles, and a number of other available objects (never teeth, though) that would accommodate the relationship between lever, fulcrum, effort, and load. Physics made fun. Because no matter where you are or what you're doing, there's always time for learning.

The travel supplies were sorted just before leaving Tennessee Tuesday morning, and we were headed south on I-75 to Macon, Georgia.

When Flem said Macon the first time he pronounced it *Macaan,* which caused me to spit up a bit of my coffee. Then he insulted me for pointing it out. It was pronounced *Maykin* every time after that. I loved hacking on Flemming for that stuff. He mispronounces a small handful of words, my favourite one of these being Popeye – he stresses the second syllable instead of the first, so it sounds like Pop-*eye.* He claims this is the proper pronunciation. I think he does it just to wind people up.

Not a single cloud in the sky on this morning. The blazing southern sun proved a worthy adversary to my hangover as it slowly made its way up and across the firmament. As soon as we crossed the Tennessee border into Georgia, which was maybe five minutes south of Chattanooga, there would be no more appropriate CD to insert into the player than Georgian native sons The Black Crowes' *The Southern Harmony and Musical Companion.* When in Rome, we must listen to The Crowes. The sun was shining, the sky was azure, and this would be a wonderfully tranquil listening experience.

I was in the back, and thus unable to control the song advance function on the player. I may have skipped opening track "Sting Me", and maybe also second track "Remedy" had I been sitting in the front. Those were nighttime songs. I needed to experience the more airy, ethereal side of The Black Crowes at this moment. Songs that could be equated with the rays of sunshine that saturated our van as it moved through a lazy Georgia morning. Hearing the acoustic intro to "Thorn in my Pride" flushed my brain with the dopamine that I knew it would.

The zenith of *The Southern Harmony and Musical Companion* listening experience is initiated by the deliberate *tik-tik-tik* of Crowes drummer Steve Gorman's drumsticks counting in the rest of the band on "Bad Luck Blue Eyes Goodbye". There's divinity inside this song, and it worked in tandem with the Georgia sun to bring me blissful peace out there on the highway. Through half-open eyes, I took in the words of the bumper sticker adorning a car in the lane next to us just outside my window – JESUS IS LORD OF ALL.

Hah. Right. *My fantasy is more significant and important than your fantasy.* Yeah, of course it is. Well, I had news for the driver of that green late-model Bonneville. Chris Robinson and The Black Fucking Crowes were the lords of the only church that mattered at that moment.

Listening to CDs in the van reminded me of that Celebrity Rate-A-Record bit that *Hit Parader* used to do where someone from the magazine, probably Andy Secher, played five or six contemporary 45s along with guys like Blackie Lawless or Neil Schon, and they provided their comments on what they thought of the singles. Shortly after leaving KISS and just before he had fully exposed his face to the public for the first time, Ace Frehley did Rate-A-Record and obscured his features by wearing shades and holding one of the 45s in front of his face for the photo. We weren't celebrities, at least not outside of the governance of this little tour. But I'll tell you that we sure could rate the hell out of a record in this van.

Next up on the player was the trusty *Van Halen II*, a record I immediately recognized with the familiarity of an old friend. I figured I'd kick off the proceedings.

"Considering the material on this record, I was always surprised that they opened it with this tune, and not with something like "DOA" or "Somebody Get Me a Doctor"," I said. I was being slightly hypocritical – I typically skip the first song on most albums, but never this one for some reason.

"Yeah. Isn't this a Linda Ronstadt cover?" Long said.

"She did it too, but it's an old sixties song. Not sure who wrote it," I responded. "But Elvis Costello and Jose Feliciano have also covered it." This was the truth.

"And also Michael Bolton. Back when he was still using his real name, Michael Bolotin."

"How the hell do you know that?" I asked.

"Dunno, man."

When I first heard this song as a kid who had just bought the cassette at a gas station somewhere in the United States during summer vacation one year, I had no idea that it was the same song that Linda Ronstadt had covered, let alone Michael Bolotin and those other guys. It sounded like a genuine Van Halen song. It contrasted a bit with the other material on the record in terms of mood because the other stuff was much more in the typical VH swashbuckling vein, and yet it never really seemed out of place.

As I listened to Sir Edward Van run through "Spanish Fly", I quietly marvelled at how effortlessly he plays such intricate material. I thought about how absurd it is that the idea of people playing his songs on YouTube is impressive, when you consider that they've practiced all those hours and come so far only to *replicate* these songs – Eddie Van Halen *composed* this stuff.

"Well, should we have the conversation?" came the question.

"You mean, who the best guitar player of all time is?" I ask.

"Yep, that's the one."

I loathe these exercises for many reasons. The biggest one is because the discourse can't be anything but nebulous based on all of the variables involved. Is it genre-limited? How do we define genre? Is songwriting a factor? Is influence a factor? Is popularity? And blah, blah, goddamn blah.

On this sunny day in Georgia during our rock and roll writers roadshow, however, I figured *screw it*. I'll indulge. Even if some of what I'm about to say may not be completely true.

"Edward Van Halen is the greatest guitar player ever," I declare. "If you like, you can name any guitarist you may think better than he, and I'll tell you why they're not. How does that sound?"

"Jimmy Page." I was expecting that one.

"Eddie was faster and his solos were more exciting," I respond. "Page was a hugely prolific songwriter and a great pioneering blues player, without question one of the true lords. But Van Halen was even more innovative. "Eruption". Followed by "Spanish Fly". Followed by "Cathedral". No contest."

I could hear Page purists all over America groan collectively as I spoke.

"Hendrix."

"Van Halen was more varied and versatile. His playing was a perfect combination of both fluid legato, like that flurry of notes that ends his solo in "Jump", and the rhythmic staccato featured in "Hang 'Em High" and "Hot For Teacher." And so many, many more." This was fun.

"Clapton."

"Hahahaha! For fuck's sake, really? Come *on*."

I had never been particularly impressed by anything Clapton had done. I knew Eddie Van Halen was a huge fan of his, but I never quite understood the Clapton hype.

"Yngwie Malmsteen."

"Christ. Malmsteen's playing was overkill. Technically impressive, but only interesting for four and a half minutes. Piano scales played through a fuzzbox, over and over again. Zero soul. Edward Van played with flash *and* soul. And he was drunk as a bastard for most of it. Beat *that*."

No further names were issued. Not even Jeff Beck's. Not sure what my retort would have been to that one. I was kinda hoping Ace Frehley and Vinnie Vincent would have come up, but they didn't. This was likely for the best.

⌒🙂

It was early afternoon when we finally reached *Macaan*. I was thrilled about all of this, absorbing the culture of all of these new places. As the standard routine was to locate the venue and then find a cheap hotel within proximity, we sought out The Hummingbird Taproom first and then the nearest Days Inn. And then some form of lunch place near one of these.

The Hummingbird was an impressive place. It wasn't open for business at the time we arrived, but it looked massive from the outside. In front of the building sat a wooden easel that supported a chalkboard displaying multi-coloured handwritten messages:

> Tonight: Authors Christopher Long & Brent Jensen 7-9pm
>   Open Mic Jam 9pm
>   3-4-1 drinks starting @ 8pm

Aggressive booze promotion. I assumed this was regular business at The Hummingbird, and possibly in Georgia. Many questions came to mind as I studied the garish yet joyful pink and purple chalk letters. What kind of crowd would we be dealing with here? Would it get belligerent? What is my normal drinking capacity multiplied by three? Why didn't I bring my guitar? Is it standard advertising practice in Macon to substitute handbills and marquees for chalkboards festooned with loopy, flowery lettering? What if Rich Robinson showed up?

Most of these questions were moot. Given the size and anticipated patronage of this venue however, I was indeed interested in how this night would unfold.

We walked up and down Cherry Street looking for a restaurant that would suit the purposes of four scraggly-looking chaps, one of which was sporting a pink beret with matching pink Hanna Montana purse. During our stroll, a shop's signage screamed out to me from above our heads with its huge pink capital letters. The sign read, THE PINK CHIEF.

"Uh-oh, Long. Heads up. This store is ripping off your scene," I said, pointing up at the sign.

"What?! How dare they?" Long responded in mock contempt.

And just like that, the writer formerly known as Long would now become The Pink Chief. Encountering this sign seemed mildly serendipitous.

A few minutes down the street we settled on a restaurant that looked appropriate from the outside. Maybe five steps inside we realized it probably wasn't. It was close to 2pm and a large number of elderly women had gathered in this place, my guess was for tea. Smatterings of elderly gentlemen were also present among the women. All were nonplussed to learn they would be hosting our rough-looking faction in their dining establishment, led by The Pink Chief. Amid the uneasy looks on the heavily-lined faces of this geriatric contingent, the four of us sat down for lunch. Turned out our waitress shared their contempt.

It was during our lunch in this environment that I developed an increased admiration for The Chief. This guy knew who he was, and he was resilient in character. It didn't make Chief uncomfortable that the bluehairs were looking down their noses at him and his multiple bracelets and painted fingernails. He probably didn't even notice. He made no apologies, and he didn't try to be someone else based on whatever moment he found himself in. This was who he was, and while I had gathered that he was clearly a generally considerate individual towards others, he didn't seem to give a damn what anyone else thought. He had character. It took guts to do what he did, and I respected that.

⁓

Later, after much driving around and some fruitless GPS navigation of downtown Macon, it was determined that the closest discount motel was about twenty minutes away in the isolated outskirts of the city, with not much else around but woods. Upon driving up to this place, we noticed only one or two cars allotted to the parking spaces in front of each of its burgundy motel room doors. Very, very quiet indeed. And surprisingly, neither the plinking of duelling banjos nor *Deliverance* came to mind at any point. But this may have only been because the owners of the hotel were an older Indian couple. There was no other staff in sight. Maybe duelling sitars in place of the banjos then.

Our rooms were even grosser than I had expected. And the sheets underneath the crappy bedspread were pink, as were the pillow cases. And not because they were mistakenly put in with a load of red socks. They were just *pink* for some reason. I wondered if The Chief somehow had something to do with this. He must have been over the goddamn moon about it.

The bathroom was particularly unfortunate in our room. Poor Flemming must have wondered what he had gotten himself into by coming along with me on this trip. He wasn't pleased at this moment. He didn't bother to wait for the ice to be dumped into the sink; his first beer was opened and already almost finished.

"This place is like the fucking Farm," he said with disdain.

"Pretty much, yeah. Just without the earwigs on the shower curtains."

"Don't be so sure," Flem responded from the bathroom.

I heard the water get turned on as Flem attempted to brave a shower. I opened a warm Yuengling and turned on the TV, hoping that the combination of beer and MTV would somehow mitigate the smell of the carpet. Compared with MTV's *Teen Mom,* I wasn't sure which was worse.

Teen Mom's programming's latent intent seems obvious – celebration of the public failure of the dimmer witted - even if the 'real' message is that the programming is edgy reality television dealing with difficult cultural themes that America should be concerned with. My concern is what shows like *Teen Mom* and *Here Comes Honey Boo Boo* tell us about ourselves.

We've always been human animals, but the fraying of our social fabric is more evident now. Our constraint is lessening. We used to regard societal grotesqueness with a deeper diligence, and with more of a sense of empathetic concern. We seemed a bit more appreciative of the gravity of it, and we dealt with it with a greater acuity. The paradigm shift away from dealing more diplomatically with dysfunction and toward fashioning it into a form of exploitative entertainment speaks to our fascination with the triumph of lazy stupidity. I don't like that *Teen Mom* and *Here Comes Honey Boo Boo* throw coal into the furnace of dysfunction and give it power, using that same kind of rationale that was deployed in converting the *uncool* into the *new cool* in the 90s and making Weezer culturally significant.

The traditional models that defined what we understood social aspiration and betterment to be are inverting themselves. And all of this illuminates what we are at our core - Darwinian animals participating in a more sociologically evolved form of natural selection. We've always been animals, but now we're animals with flimsier standards. The jester and the fool are still entertaining the king - the only thing that's changed is that this entertainment is now available on your smartphone in high definition.

When I changed the channel, I heard what sounded like Flemming having an extended coughing fit from the shower. The noise continued and I turned the TV down to ensure that he wasn't choking to death or something in there.

Ah...nope. No choking. All good.

Crystal was throwing up.

Years ago I had given Flem the nickname Crystal, because he suffered so badly from his hangovers that he would be left absolutely shattered the day after a night of drinking. He shuffled around hunched over, his face a pale green with red, watery eyes and a hilarious grin. He was so fragile looking that if you touched him, he may break into pieces. Crystal was a perfect moniker for this reason. And because it was a girl's name too.

Crystal was almost as fun as Drunk Flemming. The first time I witnessed Crystal was in a restaurant a few hours after we had woken up from a bender the night before and headed home from the party we'd been at. I had just met Flem for the first time around that period, and I had no idea how truly agonized he was by his hangovers. We all piled into a booth at the restaurant and he ordered a Caesar salad. When it was placed in front of him, the smell of it initiated his flight response and he ran to the bathroom to spend the duration of our lunch there. He got the Crystal nickname after a couple of those capers.

Flemming is known to indulge in a hangover remedy that he calls *going back to the womb*. It involves immersing himself in water for extended periods, be it in a pool, a bathtub, shower, whatever. I figured that this was what he was doing in the shower on this day in Macon. After a while I heard him turn the water off, and he came out of the bathroom in a towel shaking his head in disgust.

"How was the womb? I didn't realize you were that hung over," I said to him.

"I'm not."

"Didn't sound like it."

"That wasn't from being hung over," he answered. "Before I got into the shower I got my toothbrush out, put toothpaste on it, and put it on the pile of towels just outside the shower so I could brush my teeth in there."

"*Right...*" I wasn't sure where this was going.

"Then I reached out from inside the shower and grabbed the toothbrush. As I brought it up to my mouth, I saw a huge clump of black pubic hair stuck to the toothpaste. I started puking."

"Because there was pubic hair on your toothbrush or because you anticipated that the pubic hair belonged to the older lady at the front desk?" I had to ask.

"The lady" Flem gurgled, visibly shaken. Poor chap.

I would definitely be sleeping on top of the covers that night, in favour of getting under the putrid pink sheets of my bed.

∿

We decided to leave the motel room door wide open in favour of the aromatics of our room, thus forfeiting the ability to play the 'come on in' game with The Pink Chief. We could always resume in the next city though.

"When do you guys want to leave?" Chief inquired from our doorway. Jesse was skateboarding the expanse of the empty parking lot behind him.

"If we're twenty minutes away, let's leave at 6:30," I said.

"We should leave a little earlier, just to make sure we get there in enough time to get settled and everything."

'Everything' meant pressing the flesh and bullshitting everyone about the image we were trying to keep up. I wasn't big on getting there too early and sitting around like a monkey before start time so that people could stare at me.

"But, Chief" I asked, "what about artistic mystique?" I loved that I could wind him up without making him angry. I was lucky that he was such a tolerant individual.

"What do you mean?"

"I mean that the artist should maintain a certain amount of mystery that would be compromised by arriving at the venue too early. We should be seen for the first time just as the event begins. Mystique sells, man. Come on, we both know it."

I was just talking shit, pushing the envelope just a *little* farther to see how far it would go. In theory my postulation was correct, but I knew the reality of our situation was that we were very unglamorously schlepping our own boxes of books in and out of these venues. No roadies, no handlers. And no mystique. But I still didn't care for the pre-event pontificating chit-chat though.

The Chief stroked his chin as Jack Nicholson would have when faced with this situation.

"Mystique. There's nothing I don't like about mystique" he said, like Mystique was some stripper from Biloxi. "But tonight we're going to have mics, and we should arrive early to help set all that stuff up."

"Alright, you win," I responded. "Six fifteen."

"Seeya soon," Chief said as he turned to leave our room.

Flemming looked over at me as he switched on *16 and Pregnant* with the remote. "Six thirty."

⌒◦

The Hummingbird was a cool venue, a long cavernous hall with high ceilings and a massive bar. When we arrived, we saw that the stage at the back of the room was set up with a large table, two chairs, and two microphones. I was impressed. Chief and I hauled our boxes of books up to the stage and set up shop, side by side. Within minutes, Flem placed a pint on the corner of the table and walked back down the stairs to his seat in front of the stage, where he chatted with some of the folks gathered in a dim corner beyond the brightness of the stage lights. We had joked about him being my manager during this trip, but it turned out to be more than just a joke - he was always right there, always stepping up, supporting and contributing to the shaping of this thing as it took us from town to town. And he showed so much tolerance in doing it. I couldn't have been more pleased that he was there. Those of us who call Steve Flemming a friend are distinctly privileged to do so.

As we sat up there on the stage after start time The Pink Chief took the lead in working the crowd, leaning into his mic to talk up the books and engage the crowd in some chat. He had definitely done this before. After some chat, he read a small portion of his book. When he was done he encouraged me to do the same. I paraphrased instead, just because I think public readings are too stilted. I just feel like it's not the right thing to do. The idea of a book reading has always seemed unnecessary to me, no matter who you are. At this level (or any level, for that matter) I don't expect to be able to go into a room of strangers and have them listen to me read my book to them. I felt like it might be more interesting to talk about stories from the book, like people would relate more to that. It's more engaging and conversational that way. So, rather than read a snippet from *No Sleep 'Til Sudbury* I related a story from the book instead.

The crowd was thin, and it seemed like these people didn't quite know what to make of us and what we were doing in their bar. This was the *South*. At least for me it was, anyway. There may have been twenty-five people in the bar, if that. Each member of the female contingent seemed to be a newfangled version of Trisha Yearwood. These women all stood solemnly alongside their humourless male companions, watching us in silence. We were very much out of place in their establishment, and even more so under the circumstances that had placed us there on that night. I felt like we had an awful lot of nerve doing this.

Eye contact with anyone in this crowd was averted immediately, if not altogether nonexistent. No one would engage me visually. It may have been either intimidating or uncomfortable to have this guy from Canada in their midst telling peculiar stories about his musical childhood. I knew people were listening though, because most of them smiled at the right times. As I spoke, I was looking for a connection point. An *in*. Someone in the crowd I could interact with that would break the tension and loosen things up a bit. At the bar, there was a guy standing with his girlfriend holding a huge martini glass that was as big as my head. Bingo.

"Dude that is a *huge* glass," I said into the mic. "How many drinks does that thing hold?"

This was my Hail Mary. Catch it, brother. Come on. Catch it and throw it right back to me.

"Three drinks. It's three for one night tonight."

There we go.

"Ah, right. What's your favourite band, Martini?" Couple of giggles from the crowd. Slippery slope, though. Martini could have walked up and smashed his mega-sized glass over my head. I couldn't be sure, in this bar in Georgia.

"Pantera" Martini responded.

Damn it. No Pantera in my book. I wasn't a fan, never have been. He may as well have said Placido Domingo.

"Any others?" I asked. He started to make his way to the stage. I was hoping not to break the martini glass.

"Just Pantera," he answered.

He stood in front of the table and continued talking about Pantera, after several minutes effectively ending the interactive question & answer / book reading / story telling portion of the evening. The Chief and I just sat and listened as the very heavily-tatted Martini talked. He was well-refreshed already.

After more time had passed, I had to ask.

"So uh, did you want a copy of the book?" I took one from the neatly stacked pile and held it up towards him.

As he squinted to take in the image of the front cover, I noticed that in place of his eyebrows were instead tiny, tattooed circles. He opened his mouth to speak.

"Y'know, I'm not really into readin'. Or thinkin'. Or anything like that. I just like cleanin'," he said.

"Sorry?" I questioned.

"I just got a job cleanin' this bar," he clarified. "I just like cleanin' and drinkin'. That's my thing."

"Ah. Hey, everybody's got to have a thing, right?"

He turned to walk away. "You want a drink? It's three for one," he said.

"Sure" I said.

I could definitely use a fucking drink. Who knew what kind of drink I was going to get? Flem stepped in with another pint at that point. Bless that man.

The book signing portion of the evening was now underway. Everybody had loosened up, perhaps due to the fact that three for one drinks had started. Lots of friendly folks now. As we signed books and posed for pictures, a guy in a huge yellow winter coat approached the table.

"Can you sign this poster please?" he asked Chief and me. He had to repeat himself a few times. I could barely understand what he was saying. He was holding a copy of the promotional poster that Chief had made, that he had pulled down off of the front door.

"I'd be happy to do that," I responded. Chief and I both signed it.

"I'm going to bring it to the women's shelter and put it up there," he said.

Odd, but kinda cool. He didn't seem interested in buying either of our books, but he was very focused on having us sign this poster for him. From what I could make out, it sounded like he worked at some type of home or institution. We shook hands after signing the poster and he walked away with it. I struggled to understand his motivation in doing this, or the peculiarity of this entire situation. Here I was, some guy from Canada schlepping heavy metal books in a decidedly non-heavy metal environment in Macon, Georgia. It was bizarre for every-one involved. But I embraced it as wholeheartedly as I could.

Martini came back, with a rock glass filled with brown liquid.

"Got you a shot," he said.

"Thanks, man."

This brown liquid was clearly Jagermeister, but it wasn't a shot. It was a whole goddamn *drink*. Martini was holding one of his own, likely meaning I would be obliged to down the whole thing in one go with him.

"Cheers!" he shouted, and chugged the contents of his glass. Gone.
"Cheers." I had no choice. Down it went.

Everyone has one of those drinks that make them walk into walls, and Jager is mine. Back in my drinking days it made me piss the bed on two separate occasions. And I *never* do that.

❧

After the book signing had concluded, Flemming and I figured we'd stay back for the open jam festivities that were gearing up at The Hummingbird. The Pink Chief and Jesse also decided to stick around, and we gathered at the table Flemming had already procured. The jam was hosted by a guy who played a number of acoustic songs himself to warm the crowd up, while potential jammers settled their nerves and prepped for their own performances with the drink. When he wasn't playing, the host sat on the side of the stage and manned the sound board. He sounded great, and I started to get that tingling sensation that comes when the possibility of jumping up to play is apparent.

I scanned the entirety of the bar. The lights were down low and what I imagined were the bar's regulars were hunkered down in familiar positions, doing what they needed to do to get to where they needed to get. The background din of bar chatter and laughter was surging. The night began to take on power.

At the table next to ours sat a guy with a long, slick ponytail and a scruffy beard holding a Takamine acoustic guitar. He was making short work of the on-special PBR pitchers, preparing for his moment on the stage. We made eye contact, and I nodded.

"That's a nice guitar," I said.

He said a few words I didn't catch because of the ever-increasing noise in the bar. One of them may have been 'thanks'. I just nodded and smiled, in the same way I always do in those situations. Then he spoke again.

"Do you play?"

"Yeah, a little bit."

"Where's your guitar?"

"At home. I'm from out of town." A long way from home.

"Where y'all from?" He had a boyish, easy smile. And he was *lit*.

"Toronto," I responded.

He recoiled from the leaned-over position he was in, backing away to size me up with a furled brow. He grinned wide, and said something else I didn't hear. Then we just smiled at each other for a moment before he turned around.

A few minutes later, he ambled over to the bar and returned with a fresh PBR refill. Then he proceeded to fill my empty pint glass.

"What's your name?" he asked.

"Brent. Thanks for the beer."

"No problem."

"What's your name?" I asked him.

"Rip."

"Rick?" My hearing sucks.

"Nah – *Rip!*" he shouted.

"Ah," I said as I shook his hand. *Rip*.

"Wanna play?" He held his Takamine out to me.

"Sure."

He watched intently as I noodled a bit. His big grin signalled the absence of more than one tooth.

"Wanna do somethin' together up there?" Rip slurred. "I can get another guitar."

"Yeah, for sure man."

A short while later, a wispy individual in a long leather jacket and dark shades with short black hair came and sat down at Rip's table. An unlit cigarette dangled from his mouth. For a moment, I imagined how cool it would have been had this Lost Boys-looking character been Guns N' Roses recluse Izzy Stradlin. But it wasn't.

The Lost Boy also had an acoustic. I supposed he and Rip were jamming buddies. He didn't talk a lot. In fact, I don't remember him saying a single word or acknowledging any of us. That was okay. I kinda liked the mysterious aspect.

"You're next, Jensen," Flemming yelled in our direction. The host was getting the stage ready for the first guinea pigs. We stood up, guitars in hand. I had Rip's; he had Fake Izzy's.

"What do you want to do?" I said to Rip on our way up to the stage.

"Know any Bob Seger? "Night Moves"?"

"How about "Turn The Page"?" I countered.

"Yeah!"

Our host adjusted our mics and levels, quietly in disapproval of the number of drinks consumed at our table. He wasn't expecting much from our performance. I wasn't sure what to expect myself after that glass of Jager. Hell, I didn't even know if Rip could play.

E minor chord to start off. Nice and easy. Skeptical but curious faces at the bar. Anxious anticipation at our table. I came up the neck to play the intro lick. Rip and I nodded in unison to the silent beat we had established as we strummed. Musical language; it's a bloody amazing thing. I leaned into the mic and sang the song's first line.

The sound in this place was perfect. My voice floated up to me from the floor monitors at my feet. Rip and I smiled at each other as we continued.

Now the chorus.

I could feel it. As we continued to play, I retreated into myself for a while, to that tranquil and familiar place only accessible during times like this. The sensation is almost like being underwater. I really internalized this Georgia experience in particular, more than before given the circumstances. Seger's lyrics were narrating my current situation to me as they flowed out of my mouth. As I sang the words, I explained my own deepest, most secret ethos to myself.

More heads nodded slowly in the crowd. The slow, tender transformation was in progress.

Towards the end of the song, I looked over at Rip. He had taken to sitting down on the stage, drifting away. His chords came a bit slower, rougher. He was in his own little world too. He may have had too much to drink. I wasn't sure how much more he had left to offer musically.

And then with the release of that little signature lick, played on the saxophone in Seger's rendition of "Turn The Page", the magic concluded. We were finished. Seemed so quick. Man, it's so incredibly hard to turn that stuff off once it's been switched on.

I went back to the table. After another couple of drinks with Flem, the host came over and asked if I wanted to do something else.

"Absolutely" I responded, and made my way back to the stage.

The reason I learned to play guitar as a kid was to get closer to that special sanctum inside my favourite songs. And that journey to get closer and closer never ends, no matter how old you get or how long you play. And now, again, it was time to try to get a little closer still.

Now, there are intricacies involved. The *cut* - that special sweet spot you find when you're drinking and playing - comes somewhere after drink five but before drink ten for me. This is where the magic and the glory happen. The wind and the tides are in full command during this period. After that tenth drink, the lyrics may be partially forgotten. Embarrassing sloppiness ensues. The wheels begin to fall off, and the guitar must be removed and hidden away in a location where it cannot be found. Of course, this measurement is personal and varies by individual. I can't imagine what Ronnie Wood's sweet spot would be before he gets too messy, although he likely operates on a completely inverted framework altogether. Dude's from another planet.

At that moment onstage in Macon, I felt like I was still in the cut. I would find out whether this was accurate as I attempted the opening guitar line to Bon Jovi's "Wanted Dead or Alive". It was always an appropriate gauge for measurement.

Turned out I was closer to the end than I was to the beginning. No worries though, as the most important aspect of "Wanted Dead or Alive" is the opportunity for audience interaction. Like The Crowes' "Hard to Handle", it has a bona fide sing-along chorus. It's no secret that anybody who actively listens to the playing wants to sing. With the proper encouragement and in a safe environment, eight out of ten people will do it. The ninth and tenth persons will always want to throw a bottle at you for calling them out and drawing attention to them, even though they still secretly long to belt it out at the tops of their lungs.

In the case of "Wanted Dead or Alive", that particular part of the chorus after the first line, and right after JBJ sings "wanted...", is the precise moment for audience interaction. Those familiar with the song will know that Bon Jovi guitarist Richie Sambora actually sings the second "waaaaan-teeee-eeeee-eeeeeee-eeeeed" in between Jon Bon singing "wanted" and "dead or alive", which makes it even more perfect, because the crowd almost feels an obligation to chime in with that specific part while the performer continues to sing the remainder of the song. When I've played this song for audiences in the past, I usually sing all the parts in the first chorus, but I watch for the enthusiasts in the crowd who sing it or even mouth the words. The second time, I point to one of those people (depending on their level of enthusiasm) after singing the first "wanted...", and then they sing it. The third time, I put my hand to my ear a la Paul Stanley during that part and the ensuing magic courses through our bodies.

Sometimes.

Other times, as on this night, you're mostly just playing for yourself. The stage and the lights far outsized the crowd here in the Taproom, and as the "Turn The Page" lyrics go, I literally did feel a million miles away up on the stage. You know that the people are out there, but their shadowy images are obscured by the stage lights shining in your eyes. The distance feels more real than implied. But this just adds to the beautiful lull of the moment.

I would have been remiss to not play some Crowes during this time spent in their home state. I looked over at the emcee positioned in the darkness on the side of the stage, sitting quietly with his guitar in his lap, and I played the first line of "She Talks To Angels".

"Know that one?" I asked.

Of course he did. In response, he strummed the chords of the main part. And off we went, wordlessly.

When you give yourself to a song, there's really nothing else like it. It's an opportunity to experience complete clarity, as if in a vacuum.

The noise is washed away, and all that's left is the chance to know all the answers all at once, from miles and miles up above.

And then, at those times when you realize just how close you are to where you're trying to go, emotionality will choke some of the words in your throat as you try to sing them, because you just can't take it.

You will never feel more alive than during that moment.

Never.

Eight

Saskadelphia

~

When I awoke, the first thing my mind worked to figure out was my location. No matter how much you move around from here to there, you never quite get past that initial moment of opening your eyes and wondering why you aren't in a more familiar place upon waking from whatever dream you may have been having a millisecond before.

One more infinitesimal moment passed before my brain had worked out the first mystery and progressed to the second – why I had betrayed my own interests in sleeping above those pink sheets in that hotel room. I looked down. Thick as thieves the sheets and I were, me in my underwear and they in their resplendent...*pinkness*.

I craned my neck to the right to look at the other bed. Flemming was a wiser man than I. There he was, still in his clothes on top of the sheets, held fast in suspended animation. I remembered him ending up in that same position some hours ago, before the morning light replaced night's blackness outside our window. The only difference was that the can of Pabst Blue Ribbon he had been clutching in his left hand had come to rest sidelong on the floor beside his bed, having given up its contents to the carpet. It wasn't the first time that had happened in there.

The night before, I had come out of the bathroom in our room to notice that Flemming's eyes were closed. I called his name quietly a few times as he sat motionless on his bed, but he didn't respond. I didn't want to acknowledge at that time that once the eyes close, even for just a brief moment after a night like the one he'd had, they would remain that way until morning. Sleep had engulfed him like quicksand.

The events leading up to that moment played out in my mind like random sequences in a Tarantino movie. The one I dwelled upon the longest felt like it may have been a dream at first, but I'm sure it wasn't. As we walked past an ambulance garage after leaving the bar, Flem approached one of the ambulances parked just outside the garage. He removed his shirt, opened the door and hopped in, lying down on one of the stretchers. When an attendant ran out of the garage towards him and started yelling for him to get away from the vehicle, he clutched his bare chest with both hands and winced, complaining of a heart attack. After a minute or so of this he stood up, reached for his shirt, and jumped out of the back of the ambulance laughing, and we continued on our way.

Then the next sequence.

The memory of coming upon a restaurant somewhere on what was likely Cherry Street or somewhere nearby, where we decided some food would fortify us for the rest of the night ahead.

I asked the young female hostess standing at the front of the restaurant what type of food they specialized in.

"Tapas," she replied politely.

"Topless? I LOVE TOPLESS!!" Flem yelped, much to the dismay of the patrons of this establishment.

Funny bastard.

"Wake up, Doctor Flemming," I called over. "Time to get outta here."

"Thought you'd never ask," Flem grumbled as he worked to steady himself on the bed before attempting to stand.

Over Flemming's shoulder, a bespectacled face framed by a hand on either side of it peered at me, pressed up against the other side of our window.

"Come on in," I gestured to The Pink Chief.

The doorknob sounded. *Klik-klik*. Locked.

"One day he's going to just lose it and kick you in the nuts for that, you know," Flem's head said from underneath a towel.

"He would never do that. He's a man of the church," I responded as I let The Chief in. I wasn't so sure.

"Never gets old, huh?" Chief said with a smirk.

"Not yet, buddy." I slapped Chief on the back.

"What did you guys get up to last night?"

"Flemming tried to steal a school bus," I answered.

"Interesting" Chief said, nodding his head. "You guys ready to head out?"

"Think so. Flem?"

"Only if I can take the sheets with me," Flem responded.

"Don't forget your toothbrush," I said.

Flemming snickered, the towel still on his head. "It's garbage."

⌒○

We packed up and drove to the Gas & Sip or whatever that day's gas station combined with convenience store was called here on the outskirts of Macon, and continued our established morning routine. Coffee, portable food, liquids for the drive, and beer for that night. Being on this tour captured the beauty of living in America in free hand. We moved across the country like gypsies, free from the albatrosses of religion, politics, and overzealous lawyers hanging overhead.

Of all of the songs that romanticized life on the American road, at that moment The Tragically Hip's "Last American Exit" came to mind first. Superficially because of the fact that we were snaking along the highways of the United States, but also likely because Canada was on my mind. The Hip, as they're more popularly known in Canada, are a band from Kingston, Ontario who achieved the height of their popularity in the early to mid-90s (although really only in Canada). "Last American Exit" was their first quasi-hit, a song that was more or less nondescript within the contemporary Canadian music scene in the late

80s. But two things were remarkable about this band. The first was their unlikely metamorphosis from being a group that released songs like "Last American Exit" and "I'm a Werewolf, Baby" on their first album and sounding more or less like every other Canadian semi-popular rock band in the late 80s, into superclever musical statesmen who would literally come to be known as nationally symbolic based on the average Canadian music fan's sheer adoration of the band. The second thing was how flagrantly this nationalistic connotation prevented them from becoming popular south of the border, regardless of any consideration of musical quality and artistic sophistication.

On the surface, the first point doesn't seem remarkable. Several other artists have released debut albums that weren't necessarily indicative of their future successes – Bon Jovi, The Temptations, Supertramp, The Eurythmics (their first album, released in 1981 entitled *In the Garden*, was a huge dud). But these bands simply fine-tuned what they offered on their debut records into something much more commercially viable. Their transformation was more linear and comprehensible. Commercial success is quite different from artistic sophistication, which is evident mostly in lyrical quality and musical composition and instrumentation. It's clear that these things can be easily acquired in the music industry with the hiring of professional songwriters like Diane Warren or Desmond Child, but ultimately the inclusion of these elements trend more towards commercial vapidity and away from real musical integrity.

The Tragically Hip's success in Canada grew steadily through the release of their second album *Up To Here* and third album *Road Apples*. *Up To Here* demonstrated a drastic development in the band's musicality with songs like "38 Years Old" and "Boots or Hearts". The improved song quality allowed the band to elevate themselves above the rest of the Canadian music scene, but it was really the lyrical content that set the band apart from their Canadian peers. The band's main lyricist, Gord Downie, was like a Canadian Jim Morrison, shaman-like in his improvisational performances that could, and often did, go to places unexpected during Hip shows. Downie referenced Canadian historical figures like Jacques Cartier and Tom Thomson, and namechecked lesser known Canadian towns like Sault Ste. Marie and Bobcaygeon in his descriptions of Canadian geography. Downie's sharp, sly lyrical prose also noted sensitive Canadian sociopolitical issues, like escapes from Millhaven maximum security prison and the story of David Milgaard, a Winnipeg-born man wrongly convicted of the grisly rape and murder of a Saskatchewan woman. Canadian rock music fans seemed to buy into the fact that these songs, which initially qualified as being sonically good, contained lyrics that could make the songs substantial totems of their own patriotic opportunity. Not goofy, not cheesy. Not formal. It was something young Canadians could get behind; the cultural identity formed being one to finally be proud of. It was Canadian heritage legitimately transmuted through very legitimate rock music. Canadian rock music fans wore The Tragically Hip like a badge.

This leads us to the second remarkable thing. Despite the quality of their songs, The Hip were never able to gain significant popularity in America beyond border cities like Buffalo and Detroit, because the band was perceived as being *too Canadian*. It wasn't that the band had an overly provincial attitude about Canada as it related to the United States, because some of their songs, like "New Orleans Is Sinking", obviously reference America. But these references are only made thematically, and not in any kind of celebratory detail. The Hip's pivotal record *Road Apples* was originally entitled *Saskadelphia* by the band, but this title was vetoed by the record company for sounding too Canadian. The band then sardonically suggested *Road Apples*, a reference to frozen horse droppings, and the record company liked it without realizing the true meaning behind the local slang. Regardless of the album title, The Tragically Hip's patriotism still shone through, leaving most American audiences nonplussed.

My pal Garvey completed his post-undergrad schooling in Massachusetts and Tennessee. While he lived there, he played Hip records for the rock fan friends that he lived with, to a reception of crickets. Fellow Canadian Dan Ackroyd stickhandled the band into the musical guest spot on *Saturday Night Live*. Still nothing. In the eyes of

America, the band *was* too Canadian; but they were also too talented not to be taken seriously, and thus could not be marginalized as a satirical blame-it-on-Canada sendup and liked even 'ironically'.

Yes, other Canadian bands have cracked the American market – Rush, The Barenaked Ladies, and Neil Young are a few examples from a decidedly small artist group. Celine Dion also won the hearts of Americans, but we don't need to talk about that here.

At the time of their American acceptance Rush was recognized for their prog-rock musicianship, and not at all for being Canucks – most people didn't even know they were Canadian. Hell, a lot of Canadians didn't know Rush were Canadian.

Neil Young makes mention of Canadiana in his songs, but these mentions are eclipsed by his renown for naming his songs after American states like Alabama and Ohio. Despite the intended call-for-reform messages in the lyrics, the songs seemed to be romanticized as American history lesson glorification, and the intended message became ancillary. At no other point was this more clear than when Lynyrd Skynyrd initially called Young out by name in "Sweet Home Alabama" for his pointed references to slavery in the American South in "Southern Man", but then wore Young's tour t-shirts while Skynyrd performed "Sweet Home Alabama" live.

The Barenaked Ladies slogged through Canada for years in the same way The Hip did and finally achieved mainstream American success with the release of single "One Week", in which they rap catchy verses and touch on several hallmarks of American popular culture – Leann Rimes, Snickers, and Harrison Ford among them. The liner notes lyrics for "One Week" also contain additional lines referencing *Star Wars*, even though the lyrics do not appear in the final version of the song. Co-founding Barenaked Lady Ed Robertson decided to include them with the album notes even though they were left out of the song. The band may have tried to retain their Canadianism somewhat with a Swiss Chalet nod and the cheeky inclusion of a distinctly Canadian reference in the "One Week" lyrics, right at the very end of the song. The last line is *"Birchmount Stadium, home of the Robbie"*, which is a tribute to a sports facility in Toronto which hosts an annual charity fund-raising soccer tournament called The Robbie in honour of three year old Robbie Wimbs, who had been diagnosed with Cystic Fibrosis. The reference would remain cryptic – the song was released in 1998, while the Internet was still relatively neophytic and Google couldn't be called upon to decipher the line's meaning. Most Americans likely thought the reference was a backhanded shout-out to Florida's old Joe Robbie Stadium anyway.

Granted, when the art is substantial it carries cultural heft. In the case of music, an element that makes The Tragically Hip so special to its fans is not simply the music alone, but the music as a component of the experience of feeling patriotically involved. The Hip wore this partisanship exclusively on their sleeves, making it impossible for them to be embraced by America. Conversely, when music is vapid and impersonal it's not a problem – Justin Bieber is a full-fledged Canadian kid who grew up in Stratford, a few hours southwest of Toronto. But there's virtually no indication of this fact anywhere in his breezy pop hits catalogue. And America likes it that way.

America doesn't want any Canada. America is hard wired to only want more America.

✳

Even though we were pretenders at the road dog game, we were playing out the role with zeal as we moved from city to American city. I was, any- way. I scoured the concept of our little travelling roadshow for any trace of romantic affectation I could wring out of it. We wouldn't be doing it long enough for it to really give rise to any substantial tragic hero-type stuff. Or long enough to develop any significant tensions, paranoia, or neuroses that would compel us to contemplate killing each other with blunt objects. This little sojourn would only last for one week, and it was a fun little make-believe rock and roll touring exercise. It would be best to accept this as amateur and enjoy things for what they are. Any romantic affectation would mostly be manufactured inside my head.

I stared out the window and watched America go by. Before any of the van CDs that we hadn't already listened to went into the player, the radio was on for a bit. The deejay clarified that we had been listening to 30 Seconds to Mars, featuring Jared Leto's hyperemotive vocals lamenting his silly first world problems. Before that, noted pee drinker Kesha sang whatever her latest hit was.

Kesha is someone who furled my brow for a very brief period at the beginning of her career, just after her first hit "Tik Tok" started getting heavy airplay. Her voice had an interestingly quirky aspect to it that was removed from any measure of singing quality - it was a combination of the timbre of her voice and the way that she enunciated the words. This was the initial gimmick; her point of difference in my mind before I had seen what she looked like, or had any idea of what Kesha was even really about. I had no idea she was an aspiring Lady Gaga. I had only heard the voice. That was it, and that was enough. I thought I was satisfied with that.

Later on I had seen Kesha perform "Tik Tok" on *Saturday Night Live*, the great equalizing force in live musical performance. Watching musical guests on *SNL* is a lot like watching someone walk a tightrope without a harness – the artists are made vulnerable in a stripped-down live setting and it humanizes them significantly, often beyond the safety that gimmickry and manufactured sexuality can provide. Something about the way Kesha's *SNL* exposure posed a distinct potential for her failure made me think I had a greater sightline into understanding her for what she may have really been. Kesha didn't seem to need all of the peripheral crap. I thought I liked her without it.

When I later learned about all of the Miley Cyrus-ish cultural static that had surrounded Kesha, my interest waned. This was largely because most of this static was of Kesha's own making, and it all just seemed dumb. I made a point of not buying into it. She seemed overly capricious and artificially bizarre, becoming known for her outlandish quotes: *"I destroy men on a weekly basis. I'm like a praying mantis. I let them fuck me, and then I eat them."* Before I read that quote or had seen pictures of her, or knew about some of the unusual things she claimed to do in her spare time, I believed my intrigue was simply attuned to the unique sound of Kesha's voice. It reminded me of the time I first heard Toni Basil singing "Mickey" in 1982.

Then I started to think about the similarities between these women, and how Kesha is a distant but natural pop cultural descendant of Toni Basil. Katy Perry is too, but she's immediately interesting for other reasons; perhaps the only non-sexual one being that Perry named her cat Kitty Purry. So clever. I would have never come up with that.

The element of sex may seem peripheral to the central work as it relates to all of these figures, but it's really not. With both Toni Basil and Kesha, the initial intrigue comes with that vocal delivery that's a bit left of centre. But both also used the vocal to deliver lyrics that were packaged in varying degrees of sexual innuendo. Basil's cheerleader vocal squealed at precisely the right time, during the singing of that cryptic rhyming couplet in "Mickey" that seemed to hint at a sexual practice that's considered illegal in some parts of the United States (pretty heady stuff in '82). Many years later, faced with a generation that's much more difficult to shock, Kesha is closer to just coming right out with it - her depictions of brushing her teeth with Jack Daniel's and boys wanting to touch her 'junk' were seemingly necessary accoutrements to whoever was behind the song.

In thinking about all of this, I had to consider the harder truths. Kesha's voice had initially reminded me of a super-popified Chrissie Hynde. On the surface, this observation seemed plausible to me. But maybe by postulating this idea I was subconsciously whitewashing something with which I couldn't readily identify with something I *could* identify with, in turn making it less threatening to my aging ego. Maybe I was actually resentful that I was no longer a carefree male in his libidinous prime in a time where sex is so dramatically overt and super evident. Kesha's hypersexual image would likely be perfunctorily interesting to me if I was younger, in the same way Madonna's "Like a Prayer" video was back in 1989. Despite Madonna's intent to entangle the already hot-button topics of religion and racial tension in low-culture sexual imagery to elicit an inflammatory response, young people didn't care about whatever Madonna's 'deeper message' was intended to be. It didn't matter; what primarily mattered in this video was the potential for Madonna to bounce right out of her bra as she proudly gyrated in the foreground, shoulder straps progressively sliding further and further down her arms. The burning crosses were there in the background, but the sex was always up front. It's always been the greatest and most powerful gimmick of all. Still is. The only thing that will change is the need to manufacture deeper meaning around it as we get older.

Christ, I don't even know why I was thinking about any of this stuff out there.

⌒○

On the way to Jacksonville, we were almost halfway through our little tour. The weather was getting warmer, which was nice – if wearing a jacket in January can be avoided in any way as a Canadian, I'd take it. The Sunshine State was living up to its name during this leg. The skies were an aerial ocean of blue, not a cloud to be seen. Palm trees dotted the landscape as we barrelled down the highway, your humble narrator at the wheel. An old Jim Croce song played on the minivan radio now, one other than the two I had previously known by name - "Time in a Bottle" and "Bad, Bad Leroy Brown". I thought about how different popular music had been in Croce's day. I often had a hard time differentiating him from Cat Stevens, let alone Harry Chapin. As a casual (child) listener, I imagined all of these artists to be versions of the same, all of their sleepy catalogues blending into one another across the FM dial of the 1970s. I never really could tell them apart. Things are different now, though. Now I know that Jim Croce was also responsible for "Operator" and "I Got a Name", and that he perished in a plane crash just as he was beginning to gain real popularity. But that was then. These days, I have to worry about separating Danger Mouse from Modest Mouse, and both of them from Deadmau5.

Somewhere in the vastness of northern Florida, we stopped at a Burger King to quiet our growling bellies. The variance in available menu items in countries other than Canada always provides me with mild amusement. I'll always try something that's unavailable back home, no matter how high the potential suck factor. In particular, McDonald's and I share a distinct relationship whenever they launch their next McWhatever product. I know it's not likely going to be good, but I'll still order it anyway. I can't let it go unsampled, and it doesn't matter what it is. There's no way you can provide a quality lobster roll in a fast food setting, and yet the McLobster commands my attention. As I stared at the backlit menu boasting Burger King's offerings, I thought about the raft of McDonald's menu item experiments both failed and successful – the McRib, the McDLT (it kept the hot side hot and the cool side cool, but the outsized Styrofoam packaging required to do so inevitably raised environmental PR issues that led to the sandwich's demise). The McPizza. The Arch Deluxe, which was basically a souped-up Quarter-Pounder and one of McDonald's most devastating failures (the marketing price tag was estimated at $100 million). And the lesser-known items, like the McGratin Croquette and the McHula, a sandwich that replaced the traditional meat patty with a pineapple ring. Hard to imagine that one failing. I concluded that I can make fun of McDonald's all I want but the cold, hard grip it has had on me since my days as a young McChicken devourer remains unrelenting. The last laugh was theirs.

At Burger King in Florida that afternoon, it would be the Whopper with guacamole. This item was definitely not on the Canuck menu, and thus I predictably chose to consume that thing previously unconsumed. Of course, hindsight is always crystal clear. The Whopper with cheese would have been perfectly fine. I didn't need to go the guacamole route. It added a variant of mushiness that my hangover didn't take kindly to. And speaking of hangovers (and Crystal), Flemming was off sitting in another booth by himself, slowly negotiating his own Whopper with guac. Big mistake for him. His Whopper was winning.

As Chief, Jesse, and I sat in our booth working through our BK sustenance, a limited amount of conversation was taking place. The unspoken understanding had set in, the kind that emerges after days are spent together in a shared space isolated from the presence of others. This understanding provided a placidity that was comfortable for its participants. There was still chat, but instead of communication being entirely verbal, non-verbal cues now took the place of most of the talking. Facial expressions and body language accounted for a greater portion of exchanged information.

After our meals were more or less done, I figured I should check on my buddy Steve-o.

"How you making out over here, Crystal?" I asked.

"Not good. This burger is killing me." His hamburger bore only a single u-shaped bite mark, the cursed light green guacamole having oozed out of the sandwich in a grotesque manner.

"I liked mine," I responded. I was kind of lying.

"Fuck you" Crystal grumbled, as he worked to haphazardly remove his booze-addled six-foot-five frame from the tiny booth.

"*Hulk no like guacamole!*" I grunted, and shouldered him back down into the booth. He looked up at me and grinned. "Y'know, you're going to pay for that later."

"And what will the form of payment be?" I questioned.

"I'll think about it. We have a lot of options to work with."

"We do, eh? Got any favourites?"

"Teabag's up there on the list."

Yes, the Teabag. Testicles positioned on the passed-out individual's forehead to resemble a tiny hilarious hat, recorded in a cell phone photo session for posterity. A familiar arrow from Flemming's quiver.

"Yeah?" I responded. "What else you got?"

"I don't want to spoil the surprise for you," Crystal offered, now free from his BK booth prison. "Don't worry, you'll enjoy it."

"Whatever blows wind up your skirt, pally."

I never did find out what Flemming pulled out of his repertoire that night. I haven't seen nor heard about any photos, but it's unlikely that I was granted a reprieve. Flem was the kind of guy who ate a sleeve of Oreos in his dentist's reception area before his appointment just to wind up the dental hygienist. I'm sure he seized the opportunity.

⤙⤚

Back in the van, I took the wheel again for the last jaunt through to Jax, a couple of hours south down I-75 from wherever we were. We were reacquainted with the billboards that tugged at our primordial selves when we had traveled in the opposite direction what seemed like months ago. The tugging felt a little more aggressive now. So did the primordial tendencies.

A beat-up old silver Ford Ranger cut us off as it moved into our lane from out of nowhere. I momentarily tasted that aggression so familiar to me as a nine-to-five commuter. I pursed my lips, knuckles white on the wheel.

"Dickhead," I muttered.

"Give him the horn!" Flemming exclaimed.

"There's no point in hitting the horn other than to elicit the middle finger response. No point."

"You're just a pussy," Flemming countered, laughing. The ball-breaking inside this vehicle was nonstop.

"If I could kill people by hitting the horn it would be a different story," I retorted. I didn't really mean it.

"*Kill* people? Jesus."

"Yeah, maybe *kill* is a bit aggressive," I added. "I'd settle for lupus."

This traffic episode brought me back to the consideration of my absent alter-ego, the life separate from what I was doing here. Work Me. Work Me sometimes made me consider logic in defining the parameters of *fun*, and made me wonder if it might not be seen as fun anymore. Kinda like being in a casino; where money isn't necessarily money anymore. It's artificial. Work Me asked myself if there were correlations, and Work Me always sought answers. For the most part, I drew the curtains on Work Me and relegated him to the back of my cerebellum. No place for him on this tour.

"Time for another CD?" Chief asked from the backseat.

"What haven't we heard yet?" I vaguely remembered that there were four CDs remaining from The Pink Chief's collection that hadn't yet played. I was not interested in hearing two of them in particular.

"Here's one for ya," Chief said as he offered up his selection. The jewel case reflected the Florida afternoon sun in my periphery, further squinting my already squinty eyes. It was KISS' first release sans makeup, 1983's *Lick It Up*.

"Definitely preferable to that Pretty Boy Floyd record," I said to Chief as I opened the case in my lap.

"*Rock and roll set the night on fire!*" he responded, sampling the obviousness of Floyd's lyrics.

"I'd rather set myself on fire than listen to that CD," I said.

Lick It Up was inserted into the player, and the bombast of leadoff track "Exciter" signalled the beginning of my visceral journey back to grade nine.

This was a pivotal album for Gene Simmons and Paul Stanley. Their KISS consortium had begun to splinter as a result of the other half of the band, Peter Criss and Ace Frehley, succumbing to their pharmaceutical vices in the late 70s. The last real KISS record, 1978's *Love Gun*, had been followed by a succession of greatest hits, solo records, and live releases, and then dabbling in disco (*Dynasty*), pop versatility (*Unmasked*), and a reviled concept album (*Music from the Elder*) that made Gene and Paul revector their path into heavier territory (*Creatures of the Night*). *Love Gun* was the last *real* KISS record because it was the last one they made at their own accord – after 1978, they seemed to have lost their way and looked to their musical contemporaries for guidance. All of KISS' musical output from that point was reactionary.

Admittedly, the going was tough for KISS; from being absolute kings of the known universe in 1978 to having half of your band implode and then scrambling to retain your footing had to be pretty crappy. *Lick It Up* came on the heels of *Creatures of the Night*, the obligatory "back to basics" album that came after KISS had put their necks out on the line commercially with a sci-fi fantasy themed concept album that they were probably quite proud of, until the massive fan and critic backlash ensued shortly after its release. *Creatures* overcompensated for this misstep, the record being significantly heavier and angrier than KISS had ever been. The band would repeat this pattern again in 1992 with *Revenge*, which converted KISS' Bon Jovi-esque 80s lipsticky puckering into chin-to-chest demonic sneering, and contained songs entitled "Spit" and "Unholy". This was done in an effort to wipe away their glammy mid-80s *Asylum* (1985), *Crazy Nights* (1987), and *Hot in the Shade* (1989) follies with sinister chest-thumping scariness. As he had made a point of doing back in 1979 when the KISS Enterprise began to lose momentum, Simmons would continue to scan the popular music landscape looking for the next market to cash in on. *Lick It Up* was calibrated against the rapidly emerging hard rock scene led by bands like Van Halen, Def Leppard, Hanoi Rocks, and Quiet Riot. KISS came to the party with newish fleet-fingered guitar player Vinnie Vincent (more overcompensation) and the makeup removal gimmick (only KISS could manipulate the public by inverting the definition of a gimmick in this way).

As a fourteen-year-old around the time of the *Lick It Up* release I was still drinking the KISS Kool-Aid (Simmons owes me money for that if it ever somehow goes to market), but it just wasn't tasting as sweet as it previously had. I sipped, no longer chugged. I still nurtured my relationship with the band, digging through the *Lick It Up* record to find pieces that I could use as a newly-anointed teenager. And those pieces were there back then.

At this point, there was a peculiar strangeness in listening to this album that I'd last heard almost thirty years previous. I was a completely different person back then, one that didn't even resemble the current version of me. Neither good nor bad, just very different. I was in a van in Florida with three other people I'd met many years after that person had been left behind. This entire idea seemed novel at first, but as the CD played on, I felt a bit unsettled for some reason. I wasn't able to listen to the music objectively; only with emotional bias. The guitar solos that once seemed so immense and spectacular, the ones I used to mimic as a young kid in front of the speakers of the family stereo in full dramatic rock star pose, now seemed so small. So *regular*. I remembered that there had been magic in these songs back in 1983, but now I wasn't sure why. For a very brief moment I was confused and disappointed that I could have ever possibly thought that had been the case.

I'm sure that being in the scenario in which I had found myself at that particular time, on a northern Florida interstate, nomadic both literally and viscerally, added certain sensitivity to this position if not complication. Living in the moment wasn't enough. I had always stayed young in my mind. Sentimentality still lurked in the background, and it proved my greatest vulnerability.

It can be tragically uncomfortable sometimes, the neverending struggle between the head and the heart - the intellect pitted against the emotional quotient.

The KISS *Lick It Up* record was a commemorative emblem of something that's gone now.

And onward we go, down the road.

Nine

Wristwatch Time

~

We got into Jacksonville just before dinnertime. Really nice looking town. Sun-drenched palm trees lined the streets, and everything seemed so bright. It was definitely getting warmer. Even the quality of the Days Inns was improving. The one we found was right off the I-95 and just down the street from the venue we were at that night. Worlds better than last night's accommodations. Bigger, brighter. Better. There was also a Dunkin Donuts across the street, a definite plus.

The woman at reception was a pleasant, just slightly more than middle-aged lady whose nametag read Ellen. She was a perfect match for Flemming's charms.

"Good afternoon! How are you doing today, Ellen?" Flem was clearly feeling better.

"I'm just fine, thank you! How are you, dear?" Ellen got right up there to join him.

"I'm fantastic, young lady. Feeling chipper."

I looked at him. *Really? Three hours ago you were considering taking your own life all crumpled up in a little Burger King booth.* I loved it. Flemming was a man who led by example.

"I'd like to check myself and my friend here into your hotel if I could," Flem continued.

"Very well then, let's get started!"

These two might want to get a room of their own if this was going to keep up.

As Ellen tapped away at her computer keyboard, her engagement continued. "Where are you gentlemen coming to us from?"

"We're here all the way from Toronto, Ellen" I answered.

"Oh my. What brings you to Jacksonville?"

"Brent's a famous writer, and we're on tour promoting his book," Flem told her. Christ. Ellen turned to me.

"Would I know your book?" Ellen asked.

"Maybe. Are you familiar with *Lord of the Flies*?" I asked.

"I think so, but I can't be sure," Ellen said despairingly.

"That's okay Ellen, I'll let it slide this time."

Our room was actually inside the hotel for the first time, directly across the hall from the Long boys. The only downside to this upgraded hotel version of the Days Inn here in Jax was that there was no window alongside the door, making the 'come on in' game impossible. Phooey.

It was five-thirty or so when we unpacked whatever we'd need for that night. The signing was scheduled for seven o'clock, so there wasn't much time for fooling around. Especially with Drill Sergeant Long looming, ever interested in shaking the hands and kissing the babies of our adoring public. Still time for a few beers though. Flem completed the beer sink load-in within minutes. He threw me a warmish Sam Adams from the night before. There was a knock on the door.

"You guys ready to go soon?" The Pink Chief inquired.

"Yeah, pretty soon. The place is right down the street, so we're only five minutes away."

"Mystique, right?" Chief smiled.

"Ah, you see? You're getting it now" I said, gripping his shoulder.

⁓

The venue in which we were scheduled to appear was called Young, Loud, and Snotty, presumably named after the debut record from

American punk band The Dead Boys. It was a small hybrid music store and skate shop located in a strip mall. We appeared at a quarter to seven, backing the van up to the curb in front of the store to load in our wares. It was pretty quiet.

"*How are ya, man? Great to see ya!*" It was Jack Nicholson again, greeting the owner of the store with a huge handshake. Flem and I dropped my boxes on the table that was set up in the middle of the store and formed a pile of nine or so on the right side of it. One book standing upright, leaned against the stack, cover facing out. I reached into my bag for a couple of black Sharpies and put them on the table beside my books. Six fifty-four pee-emm. Ready with time to spare.

I looked around the store. The place reflected a punk ethos as much as a business that needed to make money possibly could. There was some cool stuff in there, some decent records. Lots of punk and metal on display, but also some blues stuff, jazz, hip-hop, and something called *crust*. Still don't know what that is. There was a *Tales from the Crypt* pinball machine by the door. Either that or *Doctor Who*, one of the two. I don't remember. Rad skateboards aplenty too. Fun little place.

Our host's name at Young, Loud, and Snotty was Dale, a youngish punk and metal fan who had opened up the store by himself two years prior. He was the only dude working at the store at that time. He didn't seem pleased with that scenario. I mentally transposed his workday obligation against mine and could not pity him.

"There's not a thing I don't love about this place, Dale," The Pink Chief intoned.

We chatted with Dale for some time about the books and what had transpired on our little sojourn thus far. Eight o'clock rolled around, and not a soul. Eight thirty. Eight forty-five. Not one person showed up for the signing, let alone came into the store. Dale apologized profusely, poor guy. He had advertised on Facebook and in other social media, but to no avail.

Nine o'clock. Time to load out and get boozed up.

Flemming and I convinced Chief to let Jesse come out with us, for dinner at least. The three of us walked down Atlantic Boulevard in the Neptune Beach district after dark looking for a place to eat. As we walked, we passed one of those portable roadside signs with plastic changeable letters. Somebody had rearranged the letters on the sign that was supposed to read *special on pants* to *special penis*. These things will never fail to make me laugh out loud. Mostly because I imagine the joker who takes the time to switch the letters around, likely laughing his ass off while he's doing it, and then admiring his work with pride in his cleverness after he's done. So stupid, and yet always so funny.

After walking for about fifteen minutes, we settled on some non-descript seafood place. It was after nine, and there wasn't much was going on. It seemed like this place was about to close, but there wasn't anything else around.

We ordered drinks and dinner, and chatted about Jesse's plans to attend college in the fall. He was excited but pensive, and I did my best Holden Caulfield in counselling him in his preparation to make the most of the experience. *Savour every minute, the time flies by - before you know it, it's over. Do your best to determine what you want out of your education before you enroll. Think about how your degree will serve you in your later life. Really think about all this stuff.* These were all things I wished someone had taken the time to tell me before I went to university. I'd definitely change one or twelve things if I could. I didn't know a fucking thing about what I wanted from school or why, until much later. I could have benefitted from added preparation. I wasted a lot of time, my own and that of other people. Hopefully Jess would pick up at least a modicum of wisdom from this barstool sermon Flemming and I were putting on at great length. He was lucky to be a kid still holding this opportunity in the palm of his hand, still in front of it. It was more than ten years behind Flem and I at this point. What I was feeling at that moment wasn't envy, but a sense of mildly vicarious hopefulness - I just hoped he would make the best of the opportunity.

After coming back to the hotel with Jesse, we dropped him off at his room and then evaluated the Wednesday night potential of Jacksonville. We cleaned out the contents of the sink while having stupid conversations that were unlimited in topical range. For example, we discussed how offensive it was back in the 70s when popular comedians or singers like Paul Williams or Wayne Newton were casted as assassins when they guest-starred on television shows like *Rockford Files*. That actually screwed with me a bit as a young kid. After we talked that to death, we went back and forth naming as many drinks as we could from those old-school Chinese restaurant paper placemat settings. Grasshopper, Harvey Wallbanger, Singapore Sling. Pink Lady. Rusty Nail. We probably named most of them, although we didn't know how many there were in total. My estimate was approximately twenty-eight. Then we talked about how irritating it was when new bands used punctuation in their names, like Portugal. The Man. Or Fun. (with the period as part of the actual name).

"What do you think the real point is in doing that, Flemming?"

"For attention and the need to be noticed," Flem responded.

"And to celebrate an appreciation for things both stupid and splendorous. It's a luxury of being young. Hey, do you think people had these same conversations when they saw that Led Zeppelin had spelled their name without the 'a' in Led?"

"Only the older ones. And they definitely did when Def Leppard got big."

"Now *we're* those crotchety old men complaining about how goofy kids are today."

"Yep," Flemming gulped from his can of Samuel Adams. "You being more crotchety and older than me."

We weren't *old*, of course, Flemming and I. Just old*er*.

Flem hadn't turned forty yet. I had. It's a weird age. You're not old, but you're not young either. It can be tricky sometimes. In your forties you're definitely older, yet still young enough and dumb enough to think you can actually cheat death and avoid growing old somehow. Passive desperation maybe.

I noticed that Flem's eyelids were getting heavy.

"Flemming, name a song that you instantly loved the very first time you heard it. A song you couldn't wait to hear again right away," I said to him.

"Uh, "Low" by Cracker," Flem mumbled.

"Any others?"

"Uhhhhmmmm... "Achilles Heel"".

"Who does that one?"

"Not sure," Flem answered.

"Never heard of it," I said.

"What are yours?" Flem asked. "I know you probably have about eighteen songs in mind, but you're only allowed to name three of them."

"Why?"

"Because your words will be wasted. I'll be asleep before you say the fourth one."

"Words are always wasted," I said. "People always use words like *awesome* or *unbelievable* as descriptors to overvalue situations. Or phrases like *that was crazy*. All of these communications are used in an exaggerative sense, diluting the real essence of the actual word."

I do this all the time. I wish I didn't. Now I was just trying to wind Flemming up. And keep him from passing out.

"Or *hate*. That one too," he slurred.

"Not necessarily. Right now I *hate* the fact that I'm going to have to leave your sleepy ass here and go out somewhere because I'm not tired at all."

"See? You don't really hate that. You're exaggerating," Flem smirked with his eyes closed.

"I hate when you're right, how about that?" I asked. Now I was just being colloquially idiotic.

No response from Flem. His night was over now. I lost him. I sat there and stared at him for a moment, pondering possibilities alone. Sleeping didn't feel like one of them. Hunting oblivion did. I stood up and began looking for one of the keys to our room.

Off I went to learn Nighttime Jacksonville's secrets, quietly pulling the door closed behind me. With any luck I might be able to find one of those Chinese restaurants with the paper placemat drink menu.

For the record, these are the songs I instantly loved upon hearing them for the first time during various phases of my life; the ones that filled me with excitement and intrigue and made me want to hear them over and over again:

"Cool For Cats", Squeeze
"Maybe Tomorrow", Stereophonics
"Goodnight Hollywood Boulevard", Ryan Adams
"Looks That Kill", Motley Crue
"Canary in a Coal Mine", The Police
"Overlord", Black Label Society
"The Breakup Song", The Greg Kihn Band
"The Writ", Black Sabbath
"Wise Up", Aimee Mann
"Don't Let It Bring You Down", Neil Young
"Kashmir", Led Zeppelin
"Two Minutes to Midnight", Iron Maiden
"Seven Nation Army", The White Stripes
"Shake Me", Cinderella
"And the Cradle Will Rock", Van Halen
"Each Coming Night", Iron & Wine
"Casimir Pulaski Day", Sufjan Stevens
"Ma & Pa", Fishbone
"Michigan Girls", Califone

Nineteen of them. Flemming was close.

Ten

Roman à Clef

~

From Wikipedia:

Preparation (edit)

A bomb shot typically consists of a <u>shot glass</u> of <u>hard liquor</u> that is dropped into a glass partially filled with beer but sometimes with some other beverage. Many variations exist.

Examples of popular bomb shots include:

- The classic <u>Boilermaker</u>: a shot of <u>whisky</u> dropped into beer
- <u>Flaming Doctor Pepper</u>: a shot of <u>Amaretto</u> and <u>Bacardi 151</u> which is lit on fire and dropped into beer
- <u>Jägerbomb</u>: a shot of <u>Jägermeister</u> dropped into a glass containing an <u>energy drink</u>
- <u>Irish Car Bomb</u>: a shot glass containing 1/2 <u>Irish cream</u> and 1/2 <u>Irish whiskey</u> dropped into <u>Guinness</u> stout
- <u>Sake Bomb</u>: a shot of <u>sake</u> dropped into beer
- <u>Skittle Bomb</u>: a shot of <u>Cointreau</u> dropped into a glass containing an <u>energy drink</u>

- <u>Hand Grenade</u>: two shots, one of tequila, one of Jägermeister, carefully balanced against each other over a tumbler of <u>energy drink</u>. The Tequila is then 'pulled' as the pin and drunk allowing the Jägermeister to fall in to the tumbler creating a <u>Jägerbomb</u> which is then to be consumed immediately after.
- <u>Pocket Sixes</u>: a drink that's passed off as an original creation by Brent Jensen and his stupid friends in bars, but is really just a ripped off amalgam of the <u>Flaming Doctor Pepper</u> and <u>Skittle Bomb</u> by dropping either a shot of <u>Disarronno</u> or <u>Jagermeister</u> into a pint of beer pre-mixed with <u>Red Bull.</u>

Okay, that last one isn't really in Wikipedia under *Bomb Shot* or *Depth Charge Drinks*. It was put together randomly at the bar one night during He-Man Philadelphia by my buddy Jammer in an attempt to give ourselves a jolt, in addition to some extended drinking longevity via the Red Bull component. Along the same lines of what spinach provided to Popeye, kinda. We told people it was a Canadian tradition, and soon we had a small group of strangers drinking these concoctions and asking befuddled waitresses for more Pocket Sixes. A crowd still attracts a crowd. But there is merit involved, because the drink can be effective – when eyelids got heavy during He-Man Nashville, a couple of Sixes were prepared and they carried us through the rest of the night. The reason we called them Pocket Sixes, I think, was because it was like being dealt a pair of sixes in poker – things could really go either way if you went ahead and played the hand with those cards. It's a pair, but it's a relatively low pair. You could win, you could lose. It was a gamble, and there was some risk involved. Just like downing one of these could just as well put your lights out for the night depending how far along you were in the game (*see* He-Man Charlotte). There may have been another reason why we called this thing Pocket Sixes, but it doesn't matter now.

Here at this bar in Jacksonville, which may or may not have been called Johnny Chang's, I asked the bartender to set up one of these little numbers and he gave me a look that was a cross between apprehension and admiration. But like any good bartender, he assimilated me and my immediate situation. After giving both myself and the person I was conversing with in front of him at the bar a visual going over, he set about his task.

This person I was chatting with was an individual named Bella. I had always supposed that Bella was traditionally a female's name. I felt like Bella wasn't really this person's real name anyway. But that was fine. There was something compellingly contradictory enough about this individual to prompt me to continue the conversation that had been initiated by barstool proximity and happenstance eye contact. Bella was intriguing, but not in any kind of sexual way or anything like that. I assumed that there would be interesting chat to be made – I could have sworn that I'd learned from our initial conversation that Bella had formerly been a worker in the sex trade.

My thoughts reached back to my university days, to a night when my friends and I were in a strip club in Sudbury. We, like most rational people, understand the rules of engagement that exist within these establishments. Strippers are not interested in you, but they *are* interested in your money. Every now and again this logic might be tested, but the general rule of thumb will typically always apply. All involved parties know what their roles are, and everyone knows what to expect.

On this particular night in Sudbury years ago, a striking young woman with long shimmering blond hair who stood maybe five-ten without heels had just finished her routine on the stage. Without hesitation, she immediately came over and sat down at our table. *Here we go*, I thought. *Time for the old erotic hold-up. Hand over your money, impetuous young fools.* But something unusual was happening. Even up close, this woman looked different. Perfect white teeth. No scent of cigarettes or booze on her breath. No deliberation in her movements, no lazy speech. Not at all like the others, on this night or any other night. There *was* no drill, no hustle. She was intelligent, maybe even sophisticated. She excused herself but quickly returned with a tuna salad sandwich in her hand, and asked if we minded if she ate in front of us as she thought we may have perceived it as being rude. She apologized that she was hungry but didn't have a lot of time to eat. She just wanted to talk. She was *nice*. And none of us were prepared for this.

As we talked, my friends and I learned that this girl was from southern California, a med student who needed money to continue her schooling. So, she had decided to take a year off school and put her good looks and charm to use in this most dubious of métiers, thousands of miles away from her other life and anyone who may have known her. Of course, we'd heard this *'I'm only doing this to put myself through school'* script before, and it was transparent. This time it wasn't. She said she had wanted to sit down with us after noting the university jackets that one or two of us were wearing. I estimated that we were roughly the same age she was. In essence, we were her people, and she was a long way from home. She was lonely and worn down, wanting to communicate with folks removed enough from the nefarious territory she was navigating as an attractive young woman who took her clothes off for money. When our conversation concluded, everyone exchanged cordial goodbyes and it was over. And there was absolutely nothing sexual (or financial) about it. It had been an encounter with every opportunity to exploit the activity it seemed to oblige, yet it was completely neutralized and rendered sexless by meaningful interpersonal exchange.

I had never forgotten that encounter, because it was one of those outliers that challenged me to reconsider my understanding of basic social construct. It's easy to make quick, prejudicial assumptions in everyday thinking, and it's so great when this thinking is turned upside down by an exception that forces you to broaden your considerations. This particular representation is a bit more charged just because of its obvious taboos, but that makes it all the more compelling. It made me wonder if I had judged the book by its cover because of some implicit danger in *not* doing so – some resistance in place to guard against the potential for any sort of emotional discomfort on my part, maybe some weakness that could be exploited.

Before this, I had often pondered the relationship between sex and psychology, always having been perplexed by the mechanical ease in which women in the sex trade were able to completely give themselves away to random strangers for money. It's not fascinating that people eschew typical social mores. We see that all the time. I was more compelled by the fact that a woman was putting the most intimate part of her physical self up for sale, and my fascination lie in the psychological dynamics at work in allowing this to happen. Was this a demonstration of great emotional fortitude, or the greatest emotional weakness? I didn't have an answer I could be satisfied with.

Thus my interest in this conversation with Bella.

Initially our interaction had begun easily enough after a very small amount of introductory circular chat. Like, two lines of it. We were both content to celebrate the sloppiness of human interaction.

"What kind of music do you like?"

"That's such a bland question. Surely you can do better than that," Bella responded.

"Okay. How about this – who's your favourite male falsetto rock singer? And skip the obvious ones." This wasn't really what I meant to ask, but it was a start.

"Hmmm. Can we open the genre up to include pop?"

"No way. That would mean including Michael Jackson, Justin Timberlake, and Weezer's "Hash Pipe"," I responded. Although, I have to admit while I'm not at all a fan, Prince did a hell of a job on "Kiss".

"Okay. I don't know, uh...Freddie Mercury? What about Barry Gibb?" Bella offered.

"I preferred when artists used a falsetto style that wasn't their typical go-to. The example I would use would be Jagger on "Emotional Rescue". It wasn't his regular singing style, but it worked," I said.

"Ah, gotcha." Bella squinted slightly. "Lenny Kravitz on "It Ain't Over 'Til It's Over"."

Impressive.

"Your turn. You started this conversation, it must have been for a reason," Bella sneered with a smile. There was no real reason I was consciously aware of.

"Nic Cester from Jet, on "Put Your Money Where Your Mouth Is". Know it?"

"Who's Jet?"

"*Come on!* Really?" I asked. "You know – "Are You Gonna Be My Girl?" *Jet!*"

"Ah, right. *Jet*. How about "Bennie & The Jets"? Elton John sings in falsetto on that last bit."

"That he does. Well done." Now we were getting granular.

"But he's singing that way almost sarcastically, in a vampy tone, so it doesn't quite count. "Bennie & The Jets" is a bit of a sendup of Bowie's "Ziggy Stardust"," I said. I was very interested in having this conversation.

"Did you know that the hand claps in "Bennie & The Jets" were inserted on the downbeat on purpose, as a sly wink to the fact that English audiences will always clap on the downbeat during a live performance?"

I did know that. I had seen a television interview featuring Gus Dudgeon, the producer of the record, discussing this fact. He said English audiences always clapped on the wrong beat and it drove him crazy.

"Yeah. I did know that," I answered, unconcerned with how Bella would interpret this answer.

"No, you didn't." Bella looked away.

"Anyway, the falsetto bit at the end contributes to the song, so it counts. That's the whole point" Bella continued, still looking around.

"That would mean Michael Anthony's falsetto harmonizing on Van Halen records would count, but it doesn't either," I countered.

Bella looked back at me directly. "You live by too many rules."

"That may indeed be true. But clearly you don't live by enough."

Bella looked at me sideways. The booze always provided a sufficient level of clemency in making comments like this one.

"Alright." Bella said dismissively, as if to wipe the slate clean and begin anew. I was quite enjoying myself, but I wondered if Bella was getting impatient.

"Who was the most recent artist to play on your iPod?" came the question. Guess I was wrong about the impatience. I was having difficulty reading this person.

"Curtis Mayfield" I replied. I was lying.

"Liar."

"Do you want me to lie and name artists and records I think you might be intrigued by, or do you want me to tell the truth?"

"I'd like to hear your lies, but then you can tell me the truth after," Bella answered.

"No" I said. "You can't have it both ways. Lies or truth, one or the other. But not both."

"Lame. Too many rules!" I wasn't sure if Bella was serious or not. "Okay. Go ahead with the truth."

"Alright. Every time you come to a party at my house, at some point in the evening you will hear M.A.R.R.S.' "Pump Up the Volume". Every single time. You will also likely hear "(Keep Feeling) Fascination" by Human League, just because of my bizarre interest in that keyboard riff. But this is not ironic, because I actually enjoyed the song when it was released in 1983, and I still legitimately enjoy it now."

Unless I had just left a party at my house, which I quite obviously did not, I did not even come close to answering the original question. But that didn't matter. All of these questions were just enablers for our loose pontification.

"Do you enjoy it legitimately, or do you really enjoy the nostalgic aspect of it?" Bella asked rhetorically.

"Both. But I was a fan then, so it's not ironic."

"You seem insistent on making that point," Bella said.

"I take the concept of musical representation very seriously. I don't like it when people try to pass themselves off as fans of a band because they think it'll pay some form of credibility dividend." That sounded a bit douchey, but I was being honest.

"That's your obsession with the irony thing then," Bella said.

"Nah, I'm not kidding around. Look at this this way - I'm not a Ramones fan. Never have been. But have you ever seen that Ramones t-shirt, the one patterned after the symbol of the Office of the President of the United States?"

"Yep."

"I love that shirt. I'd love to *wear* that shirt. But because I'm not a Ramones fan, I don't feel like I should be entitled to wear it. And so I don't," I explained.

"Bah," Bella's face screwed up. "*Who cares?*"

"I do."

The conversation paused, and we both went off to our separate cognitive corners as we took drinks from our glasses. The bartender brought over the equipment required for another round of Pocket Sixes. I winked in approval.

"So you must have seen some pretty funny stuff," I said as I plunked my shot glass of amaretto into a pint of Yuengling. I knew this comment could open the floodgates. I chugged my creation down. Bella declined to follow suit.

"Jesus," Bella said. "No fooling around, huh?"

"We say *eh* in Canada," I said.

"Well, you're not in Canada anymore."

"Yeah, you got me there. And me without my ruby slippers to click together."

"There's no place like Canada...there's no place like Canada..." Bella chanted sarcastically, eyes filled with mockery.

"Now you're getting it," I responded dryly.

"I was in Canada once. Toronto. It was beautiful," Bella said.

"And everyone was so friendly, right?" People always make a point of saying that.

"Yes, as a matter of fact they were," Bella responded. "Is that not accurate?"

"Yeah, it is. Depends where you are, like anywhere else. Sometimes Toronto can seem like a collection of opposed individuals inhabiting a common space and tolerating each other only because they have to for whatever reason. But that's me looking at it from the inside out. The opposite view, the view of the tourist, is always more favourable. All in all Toronto is a great city though; I do like it a lot. Wouldn't be there if I didn't."

There it was. The positivity. That Canadian lighthearted friendliness people always talk about. It *is* true.

As Bella and I continued to talk, I began to feel that stark solemnity that comes when you realize that your eyes are no longer working together in unison. The awareness of this fact established a mental divide that wasn't there five minutes ago. I always try to imagine that the other person has no idea that this is happening, but I can never help but wonder if the expression on my face is evidence to the contrary. Of course, it is.

"So back to your earlier question about funny stuff. I don't know if any of it was particularly funny, but yes, I have seen some very unusual things," Bella said.

"That's what I meant to say. And you realize at this point that you have to share, of course." Bella would not have reintroduced this topic otherwise. There would be sharing.

"Of course."

Bella's eyes searched the room, mentally sifting through what could be shared and what could not, and how.

"There was this person once, who just wanted to play with my feet," Bella offered.

"That's it, nothing else?"

"They wanted to suck on my toes."

"I see. You probably have a couple of foot fetishist tales, no?" I could never really figure out the feet thing myself.

"Yeah, lots of that. But that's not really weird."

I paused on my barstool, struggling with the validity of that statement.

"I've had people cry during intimacy," Bella said.

"Why?" I questioned. Two or three jokes ran through my head, and I thought better of voicing them.

"Recent divorces or breakups."

This just added an additional level of morbidity to the proceedings. I was still paying attention though.

"That's jarring," I said. I tried to relate even pragmatically, but I was unable.

"Some guys talk about their mothers. And make comparisons."

I sensed that Bella was courteously offering a disclaimer through this ambiguous phrasing that would allow me to decline hearing the details of this depravity. I did.

"Pass" I said. "What else you got?" I felt like we were coming to the end of our conversation, unless there was something else that could be talked about. I wondered what time it was.

"Once a big burly construction worker-type guy came in with a backpack. I went into the bathroom to change, and when I came out he was a she," Bella said.

"What?"

"The guy had changed into a dress, stockings, and heels. Complete transformation into a woman."

"Wow!" I said, maybe a little louder than I should have. Wall of Voodoo's "Mexican Radio" blaring over the sound system ensured our confidentiality, however.

"What did you do next?" I said amusedly.

"I asked him what he was looking for, and he, or *she* I guess, said that she just wanted to talk."

"Really? No sexual activity or anything?"

I don't know what I could have meant by *or anything* within the context of this conversation.

"Nope. We just chatted for the duration. And he – *she*, sorry – spoke in a higher, more feminine voice the entire time."

"What did you talk about?"

"Girl stuff. Makeup, clothes, shopping. Stuff like that."

"Then what?"

"I left the room, and she got changed back into his clothes." The gravity of this statement was crystallized in Bella's phrasing.

"And the voice?" I asked.

"Back to masculine."

Interesting that it was not *back to normal.*

"And walked out just like that?"

"Yep. I looked out the window, and he got into a beat up old Ford F150 and drove away," Bella said.

"Christ. These people could be my neighbours," I said.

Bella looked at me.

"These people could be *you*."

I felt the incredulity of this statement pass through my chest and out my back until it was gone away. A moment or two after that, I responded.

"Nah. Impossible."

Bella leaned forward, looking into my face. "Why?"

I smiled.

"Because I would know."

We both laughed and laughed.

Eleven

Leftover People

~

Because we were already in the state of Florida, it felt like most of our travelling was finished with. We'd already driven more than a thousand miles in the van from Orlando to Chattanooga and back down again. Now we only had about 150 or so miles to go - just two more hours down the Florida coast to Melbourne and Florida Discount Music, the site of our last appearance. With any luck we'd draw a couple more folks than we did in Jax.

Melbourne was The Pink Chief's hometown however, so the deck was stacked in our favour. He had something of a following there, and I was encouraged to see how this would play out. Melbourne was also where Poison bass player and estranged friend of The Chief, Bobby Dall, called home. During Chief's tenure as an employee of Poison, more specifically of Dall as his personal assistant on two of Poison's summer tours, it turned out that there had been more thorn than rose during their work relationship. Further exacerbating relations was the tell-all book that Chief had written about his time with the band, called *A Shot of Poison*. The book did not sit well with the Poison camp, particularly with Bobby and singer Bret Michaels. The Chief had alluded to the possibility of Dall dropping by Florida Discount Music to say hello during our appearance, and I wondered in what context this greeting would be extended. I had heard Chief in conversation with one of Dall's good friends back at the Hummingbird in Macon. Apparently Dall had sent this friend texts inquiring about the Macon appearance. I had never really been a Poison fan, and *No Sleep 'Til Sudbury* didn't exactly sing Poison's praises. Maybe Dall would consider killing two birds with one stone in Melbourne.

"He'd love your book," Chief said. "Seriously, he really would. He'd think it was funny. He may well drop by FDM to wish us well."

I had my doubts about that. Nonetheless, I'd have been interested in meeting him if he did turn up later that day.

The Pink Chief had lined up a radio interview for us that afternoon with a local rock station called WFIT-FM, and he was pretty spirited about it. I was happy about it as well, but interviews can be hit and miss depending who's behind them. Particularly in a live situation. I had done interviews before that didn't turn out as I had expected, partly because I was still learning the ropes, but also because the questions were silly and unrelated. One of my first interviews was on live radio where I was provided with a general idea of what the questions would be beforehand by the program director, only to have the deejay ask a series of completely different, more ridiculous questions live. This stuff will happen, but it distracted me and coupled with my naïveté to make for a lousy interview. But this is how we learn most effectively.

Despite our comparatively short jaunt from Jacksonville to Melbourne, the morning routine remained in place – gas, food, liquids, and beer before getting on the road. On this day though, there would be a bit more beer to commemorate the final night of our little tour.

The Chief was behind the wheel for our final trek. Immediately after he turned the key to initiate ignition, Sting's nimble bass notes from The Police's "Miss Gradenko" filled up the van's cabin as we merged onto the interstate. I really liked this record, *Synchronicity;* enough for hits like "Wrapped Around Your Finger" and "Every Breath You Take", but more so for the deeper cuts like "Miss Gradenko", "O My God", and "Walking in your Footsteps". It was a shame that Sting's intricate bass lines likely went unnoticed and unappreciated by a significant portion of the fans of this band. Sting was a hell of a lyricist too. Anybody who can pull off rhyming *Firenza* with *influenza* in a lyric deserves to be celebrated on a larger scale.

As "Miss Gradenko" continued, I considered the uniqueness of Sting's band, and how The Police never really seemed to have any musical successors mimicking their sound. This was likely because of how intricate the music was – all three members of The Police were master class musicians. The songs were rife with nuances and specific little details that most contemporary pop bands didn't bother to attempt. They played well-written songs in a punk-reggae hybrid sort of style that set them apart. I didn't think it would be accurate to describe a band by saying '*they sound like The Police*', but you could say that about 99.7% of other bands in rock history. To test this theory, I threw it out to my fellow travelers.

"Can anyone think of a band that came after The Police that you would describe as *sounding like* The Police?"

"How about Fishbone?" Chief said.

"Nah. Fishbone is pure ska."

Ska music always cracks me up for some reason. I don't know why. The Specials' "A Message to You, Rudy" especially makes me laugh, even though it really shouldn't. Particularly when you consider the punky Clash-type ethos that the band embodied. Joe Strummer wouldn't be pleased. The Clash has never made me laugh though. Just The Specials. And Manu Chao's "King of Bongo Bong", which I place in the same comedic category, even if Manu Chao is considered worldbeat and not ska.

"How about Elvis Costello?"

"Closer, but I would say no. I don't think Elvis Costello copied The Police's sound. I don't think any other band did. And Costello was a Police contemporary."

"Talking Heads?"

"Same."

"What's the point of this?" Chief asked.

"Not sure. It might be that The Police were such a highly skilled, highly literate, genre-hybrid abnormal group of musicians that no one tried to mimic them, in spite of their mainstream success. They were a completely isolated band in terms of who preceded and succeeded them. There's no real lineage. It just seems unusual when you think about it. Everything was linked during that time, across the punk, post-punk new wave, and New Romanticism genre movements. The Police were really the only band I can think of that can't quite be slotted in anywhere."

Whether or not any of us even knew what we were talking about or what we were trying to express, all we had to do on the road was think out loud about stuff like this. It was liberating.

"So you can't say something like, '*Bruno Mars sounds like The Police*'," Long opined.

"You *can*, and people perhaps *have*, but I don't think The Police launched a generation of artists, Bruno Mars especially, in the same way that groups like Zeppelin or Black Sabbath did."

"Of course they didn't. Those examples are obvious," Chief said. "Back to The Police. What about Simple Minds? Or The Fixx?"

"Hmmm. No, I don't think so. I feel like those bands were too new wavey and poppy. No post-punk spirit."

Then again so were The Police towards the end, I suppose.

"No one else really combined all of the elements the same way that The Police did, and yet they didn't seem to leave behind a legacy in terms of bands they influenced."

"But what about Puff Daddy?"

We all started laughing.

We were approaching Melbourne now.

"Sir, would you do me the honour?" I said as I passed up one last CD to Chief. It was a surprise from my bag that I had been holding onto since the CDs were first broken out at the beginning of the tour. One of my absolute favourite records - Led Zeppelin's *Physical Graffiti*.

"Ah! Where did this come from?" Chief asked.

"A gift from the golden gods," I responded in reference to Robert Plant's immortalized phrase.

"It would be my pleasure," Chief said as he accepted the jewel case.

"Throw on disc two first please," I requested. It was more of a *Physical Graffiti* disc two vibe at that moment, as the afternoon sunshine would work in perfect tandem with the more mellow material that was on the second disc – "Down by the Seaside", "Bron-Yr-Aur", and "Ten Years Gone". Disc One, which featured "Trampled Under Foot", "Custard Pie", and "Houses of the Holy" was a bit more up-tempo. Better suited for nighttime listening.

This record has it all, man. It's Zeppelin's absolute finest moment, just slightly better than *Led Zeppelin IV* based on the sheer vastness of musical output. When people have that 'desert island record' conversation with each other, they would be remiss in not discussing *Physical Graffiti*. There's nothing missing. Everything you need as a rock and roll fan is right here.

"In The Light" began to play. I became so deep and downwardly involved in this music that I almost felt like I'd turned myself inside out.

"Can you think of any bands that came after Led Zeppelin that kinda sounded like Led Zeppelin?" Chief asked.

"Nah, not one," I sneered. "No one ever copied Zeppelin."

"Many replicants, but there'll never be another band like them," Chief said in a serious tone.

"There can't be, you're right. It's all been done. It's only being redone now. It's being redone *really well* by some bands at the moment, mind you, but there can never be another Zeppelin. We live in post-rock and roll times, my friend," I said, trying not to sound too wistful. Or ancient.

"Ever wish you could go back and experience that music first hand?"

"Yeah. But if I did, I would just hope that I appreciated it in real time as much as I do now. I sometimes wonder if I tend to overly commemorate it just because I can't go back there and experience it directly."

"Y'know, it's funny. When you're young, you pay absolutely no attention to youth because it's all you've ever known. When you're no longer young, only then do you realize what you've lost. And I think people get stuck in that, and they resist forward movement. They deliberately stay behind in their lives, trying to relive their youth over and over again. They don't grow. They're just – stuck. Like leftover people from another time."

"Does steadfastly theorizing that there will never be another Led Zeppelin and that we live in post-rock and roll times mean *we're* leftover people?"

There was a weird pause.

"I'm not sure."

⤳◯

The road signs advised me that the thousand mile-plus road trip that we had embarked upon back in Orlando last Sunday was nearing its end, with only a few miles left to go. Melbourne was very close now. Our time in this van together was almost over. I tend to languish over the endings of things unnecessarily, regardless of what the endings may represent. Always have since I was a kid. Not sure why. I have a distinct concern with the passing of time, and I really wish I didn't.

Partly to relieve my mind of this distraction, and partly to prepare for this radio interview, I reached into one of my book boxes and cracked a copy of *No Sleep 'Til Sudbury*. I flipped through the pages thinking about general themes that might be interesting to discuss. There would not be any passage reading from me on the radio. As I scanned a random page, I remembered the soul-sucking endeavour that was the editing process of this book. After the editing was complete, I was so sick of the book I never wanted to see it again. This had actually been the first time I had read through it since then.

I heard Chief's driver side window go down. I didn't look up. Suddenly the van swerved sharply to the left, taking all four tires off of the highway and into the fescue on the side of the road at full speed. Then just as abruptly, right back onto the highway. Everyone was quiet for the next eight seconds, as we tried to regain composure while navigating through the confusion of what had just happened. The realization that we could have rolled the van at eighty miles an hour set in. No one spoke for the remainder of that minute. Or the next one.

I looked up from the book. "Would you give me a heads up before you decide to do that again please?" I said. The words were dismissed by everyone's ears as soon as they left my mouth, filed away. Turned out The Chief had attempted to spit his gum out of the window, and for whatever reason went off-roading as a result. Our trip almost ended before it was over. Everyone was a bit ragged at this point. But the end was in sight now. We entered Melbourne within an hour.

I don't know if it was because I knew that Chief and Jesse lived there, but Melbourne seemed like that much more of a hospitable, charming town. They gave us the spoken tour as we drove through, pointing out places they'd mentioned in earlier chat along with places they hadn't. One of the attractions along the way was the Starbucks that Bobby Dall frequented, and I craned my neck to scan both the interior and the parking lot as we passed by. No Bobby. Up until I had met The Pink Chief, the pictures that played in my head when I heard the name Bobby Dall were the black and white ones of him crawling around wasted onstage before being gathered up and escorted away by a handler in the "Every Rose Has Its Thorn" video. Now when I hear the name Bobby Dall, I just think about that Starbucks in Melbourne, Florida.

Twelve
Red Light Lit

~

WFIT 89.5 FM was situated on the campus of the Florida Institute of Technology and served The Space Coast, the region of Florida that surrounded the Kennedy Space Center where NASA launched Space Shuttles up until July 8, 2011.

None of this sounds very rock and roll at all. However Todd Kennedy, the station's program director and host of the Sound Waves show we would be interviewed on, was definitely a rock and roll guy. Chief advised that we would be in good hands.

We tuned the van's radio into WFIT as we wound through the streets that would lead us to the station. Roth-era Van Halen was playing. This was a good sign. After "You Really Got Me" concluded, Todd's voice announced our on-air visit:

"In about twenty minutes I'll be joined by guests Christopher Long, author of A Shot of Poison, *and Canadian writer Brent Jensen, author of a book called* No Sleep 'Til Sudbury. *I'm going to be talking to these guys about their rock and roll books and the upcoming appearance they'll be making tonight at Florida Discount Music. Should be a blast, stick around."*

When we arrived, we parked the car in one of the campus parking lots and scooped up a few books for Todd. As we walked across the campus, we were getting some curious looks from the kids who were on their way to wherever they were going that afternoon. They couldn't be blamed for holding their glances – the Hanna Montana bag and pink beret had likely stirred their fears.

Inside the WFIT building we met the station manager and were given a quick tour around the place until Todd was ready for us. Cool, modern facility. Nice and bright, with lots of windows that welcomed in the Florida sun. We were led into a studio with a console at one end and a large open space at the other. Todd, who was sitting at the console in front of a computer monitor and a large microphone, sprang up to greet us.

"*Hey guys! Come on in!*" he offered with a big smile. I liked him already.

Chief and I sat at the console in front of two boom microphones, and Flemming and Jesse were seated in chairs over to the side of the studio. We talked with Todd for a bit about the week we'd experienced thus far. He seemed really interested in the concept of what we were doing, touring the country in a van *Almost Famous*-like. He was a really upbeat, positive guy. Smiled the entire time. We tested mic levels and then chatted some more about the books. He and The Chief had known each other previously from the local music scene. As we talked, I realized that Todd had taken the time to read pieces of *No Sleep 'Til Sudbury* online. This would make things so much easier.

"Okay guys, you ready?"

No matter how prepared you are, or how much of an expert you can possibly be on the topic you're being asked to speak on, there will always be that last little tinge of anxiety. It never fails to emerge as you curl your toes over the edge of the cliff, one half of a second before you jump off.

Todd had cued up Zeppelin's "Rock and Roll" to play underneath the opening of the interview, and now Bonzo's frenzied snare and open hi-hat intro blasted out of the monitors. Red light lit.

"Broadcasting from Florida Tech, WFIT FM in Melbourne this is 89.5. My name is Todd Kennedy here on Sound Waves, and we have some very special guests in the studio this afternoon. We'd like to welcome Christopher Long, the author of *A Shot of Poison* and his new book *C'MON!* and also Brent Jensen, who just recently published his book *No Sleep 'Til Sudbury*. Guys, thanks for coming in today."

"Happy to be here, Todd."

"Man, so both of you guys have led a rock and roll life, I guess huh?" Todd asked. "I mean, you both sort of came of age in the 80s when hard rock and heavy metal was really coming on strong. Do you think that sort of formed your current opinions, your perspectives on things?" Todd looked at me.

"I think so," I replied. "I think that being a part of that whole movement when you're a kid, you look back on that now in consideration of how truly impactful it was, y'know, from a nostalgic point of view."

I didn't quite answer the question there. Still settling in.

Over the course of this interview, there would be a lot of *y'knows* used. I've always been interested in the fact that the use of these little verbal crutches, when not blatantly overused of course, actually sound completely acceptable during interview dialogue, and in fact make the interview sound like it's flowing as an interesting, reciprocal conversation should. Lars Ulrich was an absolute master in this area.

"Now Brent, your book talks about growing up outside of Ontario, in Canada? A small town?"

"*In* Ontario, *in* Canada."

On the radio, that delivery may have sounded snide. It certainly sounded that way to me when I listened back to this interview afterwards. But I didn't mean to sound bitchy there at all. I completely get that Florida is a long way from Canada in more than just a geographical context.

"Riiiight." Todd responded. He had never been up there before.

"Did you see a lot of bands up there?" he asked.

"I saw a couple, yeah. My first concert was Iron Maiden on their *Powerslave* tour, and that was a big thing, y'know? I got into Iron Maiden around, I'd say, '82 or '83, and I found out they were coming to my town, which was rare because it was a smaller, more out-of-the-way city in Canada, and it was a big deal. I was really excited about it."

Hah. Throw an *'eh'* or two in there and I'm Doug McKenzie. Run-on sentences also fly in radio interviews, by the way.

"One of the chapters in the book actually recounts the experience of my going to the concert, the whole run-up to the show, and y'know, what the overall experience was like and all that stuff. Twisted Sister was opening the show, it was around the time of their *Stay Hungry* record and "We're Not Gonna Take It" was the big song on the radio y'know so, it was a really cool experience."

Thankfully I didn't say it was a 'big deal' again. I was excited to be on live radio in The Sunshine State, and I wasn't focused so much on word choice.

"Right," Todd said. "So it must have been a great time, because metal was just starting to get popular, and it was exciting. There were all these new bands coming up, and you went to your local record store to pick up the latest record..."

"Todd, that was one of my favourite parts of this whole thing - hanging out at the record store for countless hours, and when your favourite bands had their new record coming out, y'know, you were right in the middle of that, and you were waiting for it on like, a Tuesday afternoon. You'd make sure you were at the shop waiting for it, and – *there it is*! You'd recognize the band's logo, and you'd hold the record in your hands and absorb the artwork and the newness of it for a minute, but y'know, you had to get it home so that you could look at the liner notes and the pictures and soak up every detail. I was absolutely focused on all of that. This was all part of the overall experience of enjoying music back then."

Sentences *really* tend to run on during interviews.

"Now, growing up in Canada, and seeing some of these metal bands, um...you had a funny quote in your book about Motley Crue's *Shout at the Devil* album," Todd commented.

I started laughing. "Well...in the book, I touch on what it was like to grow up in a small town listening to heavy metal but um, I listened to these records a lot and I provide a little bit of critique in the book too, so...y'know *Shout at the Devil*, for me - and Chris and I joke around about this since the reason he reached out to me was because he read that quote on the back of the book, but - the quote is, one of the best things about being young is that you're afforded the liberty of being stupid, and *Shout at the Devil* is a stupid record for stupid young people."

"And you're a metal fan too!" Todd said.

"Absolutely!" I responded.

Laughter broke out in the studio.

Chief jumped in. "I read that and said, *this is my guy, I gotta buy his book!*"

Then I felt the need to clarify my position. The quote isn't meant to be derogatory.

"I think that most metal fans recognize that there's an inherent cheesiness in heavy metal, that kind of splendourous stupidity that makes metal so much fun to listen to. I mean, most fans recognize that."

"What do you think the attraction is, you know, for young kids?" Todd asked next. "What is it that draws them to heavy metal, particularly in a small town? What is it about metal that attracted you to it?"

Bless this man. Todd was just lobbing up the softballs to me now.

"Well, for me, I was a big KISS fan when I was a kid, so I think that the um, visual aspect that bands like Iron Maiden and Judas Priest had was a component that went along with the music. It was almost like a soundtrack, the music was, to this visual thing that these bands had going on. Growing up in a small town, where there was a natural lack of stimulus, that sort of thing definitely got my attention. And as a KISS fan, it just seemed like a logical progression to get into Motley Crue around the *Shout at the Devil* period. I remember opening a magazine in, I think it was '83, and seeing the ad for the *Shout at the Devil* record, and it was like, Fire? Check. Leather? Check. Blood? Check. Big hair? Check. *Who are these guys??! I gotta get this record!!*"

"It was all there!" Todd said. We were all laughing.

"And right back to the record store I went, y'know?" I added.

"Chris, do you remember these same experiences?" Todd asked.

"Yeah, I remember those days very similarly. That's why I reached out to Brent when his book came out. I discovered it online and read some of the initial quotes and reviews that it got and uh, I got a copy of it and I went *holy cow, I feel like I know this guy.* He was telling my life story too. He perfectly captured the passion of loving those groups – y'know, that's what we believed in growing up. It was your *bands*, whether it was metal or whatever the genre was. In the 80s, we were passionate about the music that we loved."

"Now you had written a book called *A Shot of Poison* that talked about your tour with the band Poison," Todd said.

"Um-hmm, right, right," Chief responded. "My first book came out in 2010, and chronicled my experiences working for Poison. It was something I never would have dreamed would happen. They were one of my favourite 80s bands growing up, and I actually got the opportunity to go out and tour with them."

"You were a fan of the band before, and now you're working for the band and going out on tour. Did it change your perspective? Did it change your feeling toward the band?" Todd asked.

"Absolutely," Chief shot back.

"Good or bad?"

"Well....ahh...."

I started laughing. So did Todd.

"We'll just say that it's totally different being a fan and hanging out. Once you're on anybody's payroll, things...change."

Impressive poise. The Chief was cut out for this stuff.

"Money can change things," Todd surmised.

"Yeah. It was a drastically different experience than what I had anticipated. We'll say that." More laughter.

Todd turned to me. "Brent, did you hang out with bands at all, or were you just in the audience?"

"I would say I was in the audience. I mean, growing up where I did, it was four hours north of Toronto so there wasn't really any opportunity to um, y'know, mix. Being up there, I was definitely on the outside. I used to look in the Toronto Star at the concert listings and see that Motley Crue was playing Maple Leaf Gardens or whatever, and it was almost masochistic in a sense, y'know - *why am I doing this to myself*? I really wanted to go to these shows, but as a fifteen year old I just couldn't get down there."

"Yeah," Todd mused. "Now, Canadian bands - there were Canadian hard rock and metal bands around that time too, right?"

"Oh yeah!" came my response. Funny question.

"And you saw those guys? Did you hang out?"

"I did, yeah, I did. We didn't hang out though. The obvious ones like Rush, and I think maybe Triumph and Helix you guys may have been familiar with down here..."

"Yep," Todd jumped in.

"Anvil was a big one up in Toronto. Toronto had its own little scene that kinda resembled the Sunset Strip a bit. There were places like The Gasworks and Rock n' Roll Heaven that, y'know, I would read about in a magazine called *Metallion* out of Toronto that featured all of these homegrown bands that I followed as well."

"Is there a difference in the bands' sound, like y'know, LA had its sound and the UK had its sound, did Canadian bands have their own sound, or..?"

"Yeah, I think so. But I don't know how I would describe that sound. Um - in the book I make some comparisons between Anvil and the New Wave of British Heavy Metal, and I try to connect KISS to all of this too. Stupid fun."

This was in fact a very poor representation on my part of how Canadian 80s hard rock and metal sounded. I had lost my train of thought. But Todd was laughing at this, so all good.

"Now, what prompted you to write the book? What made you want to write those stories?" Todd asked me.

These were simply the best interview questions ever. Todd was smart enough to know what questions to ask to cultivate a relaxed conversational atmosphere. Seems elementary, but you'd be surprised. I'd had terrible interviewers asking lousy questions up to this point, so this was a joy.

"Well, one afternoon I was sitting around listening to stuff from back when I was a kid and I really got to thinking about how truly impactful this music was on my youth and my development, and about how significantly it had imprinted itself on me. I also thought about the sheer power of nostalgia. When you're a kid, and you're seeking out these stronger sensations in a sleepy little town, music can be like an absent friend. It meant everything. It was really important to me in helping me to find my way back then. I got caught up in how much of an emotional investment I made in these records as a kid, how attached I felt to this music. I thought I needed to write it all down. Surely someone else could relate to it."

"And you remember these stories?"

"I do. One of the chapters is about me going through my high school cassette collection, which I still have, and I just talk about all of these tapes in front of me. I mean, the Metallicas and the um, the Guns N' Roses tapes are in there, but there were a lot of lesser-known bands as well. I went through them all and it jogged some memories, and I recount some stories about growing up that aligned with the music on the cassettes, and all the associated hijinks and drinking capers from back in the day. It's a different kind of rock book, with much more of a personal spin."

In that bit I specifically pronounced *about* as it is intended to sound; avoiding even coming close to saying *aboot*. Like Canadians actually say '*aboot*' anyway.

"Yeah" replied Todd. "There's a funny story in the book about you meeting Gene Simmons. Can you talk about that?"

"Yeah, sure. Uh...that was actually in Toronto, and that was...I think that was probably about twelve years ago. Gene was in Toronto promoting his book that was called *KISS and*....something. Ah, I don't remember."

I wanted to say the book was called *KISS and Sell*, but that was a book actually written by Chief's buddy Chris Lendt, who used to be one of KISS' finance guys on the road.

"Anyway, so Gene is on the fourth floor of the Chapters bookstore, which is your Barnes & Noble I think, and there was this huge lineup that snaked through the bookshelves, about three hours long. So I waited and waited, and I was thinking that when I got my book signed I didn't want to be that guy who says '*I love you man!*', y'know? I wanted to think of something maybe a little more germane to say to him that might get his attention. I suspected he'd been hearing that all night already, and probably the night before, and so on right?"

"Probably, yeah," Todd nodded.

"But what I didn't anticipate was that star power that, when you're standing across from a guy like Gene Simmons of KISS, all of a sudden it can have a crazy effect on you. So, y'know, I'm about five or ten people away and I'm thinking, *what can I say?* I used to listen to KISS in my basement just transfixed on the lyrics, so I figured I would maybe quote a lyric from this song called "Great Expectations" that I used to listen to all the time from KISS' *Destroyer* record. The lyric is, *and in the din it seems, I'm a million miles away,* referencing the huge gap between the rock star and the fan. So this is it, I have it. I'm ready now. So I come up, and the guy in front of me is *crying*, and I'm like, starting to get nervous here! So now Gene and I are face to face, because he's sitting at a table on this riser and I'm standing, so we're eye to eye. I'm *dying* at this point. Then, he says in a really deep, calm voice, '*How are they treating you in line, boss?*' My mouth is open and I'm like, '*okay, thanks*'. "

"He's without makeup, of course?" Todd laughed.

"Yeah. But I mean you're that close that you see, y'know, the little liver spots on his hands and stuff like that. I was *right there*. So I said, '*Gene, in the din it seemed you were a million miles away but the world is a lot smaller now*'. Or something like that. I kinda bungled it all up because I was so nervous."

I actually screwed up the telling of this story during the interview, because I was so excited to be telling it in this forum.

"So his handler, the guy who opens the books for Simmons and slides them over to him to sign, looks at me like I'm a meth addict or something. And Gene doesn't get it - I guess he had forgotten about the song, because it was from the mid-70s and would've been considered filler on an album like *Destroyer*. So he looks up at me and tilts his head to one side and says, '*sorry man, I don't have anything that philosophical for you, it's been a long night.*' And he starts laughing!"

The laughter in the room caused the console's volume unit meter needle to shoot into the red and light the LED indicating 'peak' for half of a second.

"So then, right at the end, sure enough, Gene puts his hand out. We shake hands, and he puts his other hand on mine, looks me in the eye, and quietly says '*thank you*'. And I put my other hand on top of his and say, "*You're welcome. I love you, man!*"

The whole studio erupts with laughter. "Dammit, what did I say that for??!?!" I couldn't help it."

"*I love you, man!*" Todd shouts out in hysterics. "Hilarious! And it's all in the book, *No Sleep 'Til Sudbury*, right?"

"It is, yeah," I reply. "I think it's in Chapter Two."

"Alright" Todd said. "So - both of you guys are doing the ultimate rock and roll thing. You put out new products, and you go out on tour in support. Right? You guys have been travelling around for how long now?"

"We've been out on tour all week," The Pink Chief responded. "Uh, I connected with Brent through his book, and we sorta became pals online, and I said '*listen, we need to get together and go out on the road*'. He'd been doing his own appearances up in Canada, and I'd been doing this for the last couple of years with my books, so I said '*let's get together*'. Like in the old days, you had Aerosmith and KISS touring together, you know, the big rock and roll road show. Two rock authors, let's book some dates, let's go out on the road."

I think he meant to say KISS and Ted Nugent. Or maybe Aerosmith and Ted Nugent. But not Aerosmith and KISS. That just happened two summers ago.

Todd laughed regardless. "And travel around in a van..."

"Yeah! And, Brent is just insane enough to go, yeah, that sounds like a good idea! So, he and his buddy flew down from Toronto last week, and we met at the Orlando airport and we rented the van, and off we went!"

"There you go," Todd chimed in.

"We've been all over the southeast meeting people, sharing stories, and talking about, y'know, rock and roll, life experiences, and writing, and publishing, and it's been incredible."

"That's very rock and roll, man. I'm impressed," Todd said.

"Absolutely. We're on the club tour," Chief said dryly to much laughter. "I'm fifty - it took me fifty years to finally get to do my club tour."

"And stadiums next, right?" Todd asked.

"Yeah sure, sure" Chief purred. The guy was an absolute pro at this stuff.

"Now, you have a gig tonight, right? Do you call book signings *gigs*?"

"Hey, why not?" Chief replied.

"He calls them shows," I said. "As in, '*what time is the show tonight?*'"

"Ah, I see. So what time *is* your show tonight?" Todd asked.

"We're at Florida Discount Music at seven o'clock tonight, which is one of the most iconic musical locations in Melbourne," Chief proclaimed. "Thirty-five years ago when I was a kid our band bought a PA system at Florida Discount Music, y'know? So it's a real hoot to be going there tonight and doing the book signing."

"So both you guys will be on stage at seven tonight?"

I nodded, Chief verbalized. This was his turf. "Yeah, seven. They have a great little bar set up in the back now called Open Mike's with a stage built right into the shop. They do live entertainment there, lots of tables and chairs, lots of space. It's a really cool little venue."

"So you'll have your books for sale there? You'll be signing 'em and all that stuff?"

I knew that Todd was doing this for the benefit of the listening audience, spelling out everything in very clear detail to ensure there could be no misunderstanding this promotion, but it was still funny to me for some reason. I pictured drunken impatient rock stars standing up abruptly and smashing up the premises, the way that Guns N' Roses demolished that MTV set in their heyday. You had to be out of your fucking mind to do that stuff. Todd was doing us a huge favour.

"Yeah," Chief continued. "We've got the print copies, we've got the electronic copies, all of it. We can sell Kindles, we can sell print copies, we can sell...ice cream cones out of the back, whatever you want tonight we're going to be able to take care of you."

Had I been listening to this interview on the radio, I would have made a point of attending this book signing just based on Chief's David Lee Roth-isms alone.

"Do you have a book reading on cassette? Can I get a cassette of this now?" Todd joked.

Chief paused, but only for a second. "Gimme fifteen minutes, dude! I've got my blaster out back, give me fifteen minutes and I'll at least get ya the first chapter."

Hilarious. The VU needle stayed in the red a little longer this time.

"All right!" Todd exclaimed. He had to be pleased with the way this was going. "Well, you can see both Chris Long tonight, and Brent Jensen, the author of *No Sleep 'Til Sudbury* hanging out and talking about their books, and you can have them sign copies of their books for you at Florida Discount Music, seven o'clock tonight."

"Looking forward to it," Chief said.

Todd leaned into the microphone. "One more question. I've been around music for a long time, but...what is the difference between hard rock and heavy metal?"

"Have you read that in the book?" I asked this because one of the chapters was called 'Hard Rock or Heavy Metal?', and it focuses on the differences between the two genres. I thought he might have been referencing it. He was.

"Just parts of it," he said.

"Todd, you gotta read the whole thing! There's an entire chapter dedicated to answering that question." He must have seen it in the contents page.

"Can you pass the book over for a minute please?" I asked.

"Yeah, here," Todd said. I was so stoked to show him the chapter that it was lost on me that we were doing a radio program, and that dead air ensued as I flipped through the pages. Oops.

Todd jumped in. "So, I always thought that heavy metal was more theatrical, and hard rock is like, more in your face. This is just me winging it," he proposed. I put the book down.

"Yeah, yeah, you're right. I mean, the age old question is, is Van Halen heavy metal or is Van Halen hard rock? Is AC/DC heavy metal? Is Def Leppard heavy metal?"

These weren't really age old questions. I suspect most people care very little about these questions, in fact.

"Aaaaah, yeah...!" Todd seemed to care about this.

"Right? It's one of those things that always kind of irked me. You'll see something in a magazine that reads, *heavy metal act Def Leppard is playing the Tokyo Dome*...and y'know, it's like a pet peeve. Def Leppard is not a heavy metal band by definition. So in one of the chapters I said, listen - this is what hard rock is, this is what heavy metal is, based on a number of criterion that would constitute the definition of each. And I go through all the bands and say, this band *is*, this band is *not*, this band is *this*, this band is *that*, and so on. And I mean, a lot of it is personal opinion, but I tried to make sure these evaluations are as academic as possible in terms of the defining factors and variables that constitute each genre. For example, heavy metal is more militant and steely. More fantastical. Hard rock is looser and sleazier, it has more groove. Tempo wise for hard rock you think Aerosmith's "Rag Doll", y'know – rhythmically it's *one...two, one...two*, like that. A little more laid back."

"Yeah" Todd agreed. "I'm going to have to read the book now - that was a good answer. Really interesting!" Todd said as we both laughed.

"Brent's heavy metal and I'm hard rock," Chief chimed in.

"What's that? You're heavy metal and what?" Todd asked.

"I'm hard rock, man, yeah," Chief replied.

"And he's metal?" Todd nodded in my direction.

"Yeah," said Chief.

I had no idea where this line of reasoning was coming from.

"The chicks dug the hard rock a little bit more, so I stayed more over to the hard rock side of things." Chief inferred.

"Did they?" Todd wondered.

"Yeah," I agreed. They probably did.

Todd was skeptical, or just trying to wind Chief up. "You don't think the spikes, y'know, on your neck and all that, did it for the girls?" he asked.

"Hey, that still has its appeal I guess." There were multiple conversations happening now, peppered with giddy laughter.

"The Judas Priests and the harder-edged bands kinda got more of the guy following, and the Def Leppards and, y'know, the Poisons and Bon Jovis got more of the girls. That was the side I tended to gravitate towards," Chief said with Diamond Davey deliberation.

"Man, I am so glad you guys came in. I learned so much today!" laughed Todd. "This is great. We're speaking with Chris Long, the author of *C'MON!* and *A Shot of Poison*, and Brent Jensen, whose new book *No Sleep 'Til Sudbury* is out now. They're gonna be at Florida Discount Music tonight at seven pm, right guys?"

"Right," said Chief. "It's gonna be a gas."

"Thank you so much for coming in guys, it was a lot of fun."

"Our pleasure."

"And I learned something today too!" said Todd. Todd's enthusiasm made this so much more enjoyable that it could have been.

"That's very important," I added.

"You're a smarter man now," Chief remarked.

"Alright guys," said Todd. "I love you, man."

That was clever. I didn't catch that comment until I heard the interview played back later.

"You're listening to 89.5 FM WFIT in Melbourne."

Thirteen

The Boy Who Didn't Get His Ice Cream

~

The next few minutes of driving from the radio station to Jesse's mom's house in Melbourne would be our last as a travelling collective – Jess would now expatriate himself from our band of gypsies. He was a thoughtful kid with a big heart. I had worried before the trip began that he would loathe being in the close company of three men removed from him by a generation, two of whom he had not previously met, but he proved me wrong in a big way. He was relatively quiet for most of the trip, but my awareness of him was shaped more through his non-verbal contributions of consistent support and patience, and a demonstration of maturity as this thing unfolded itself as ramshackle as it had over the course of the week. This trip had provided him with every opportunity to conduct himself as a teenaged stereotype; a lawless, snotty little motherfucker, particularly since it could be argued that we were more or less conducting ourselves in a similar way. But he didn't.

As we unloaded Jesse's bags for the last time from the vessel that he had spent a considerable portion of his past week in, he invited us into his home to show us his room. Flemming and I followed him through the front door. The Pink Chief hung back and reorganized the van's baggage.

Jesse lived here with the longhaired couple whose framed photographs prominently occupied the walls of this home, his mother and stepfather. Tributes to KISS, Led Zeppelin, and other bands of the era in the form of framed album covers shared wall space in the living room. Some of the frames were empty.

"Work in progress," Jess explained as he nodded in their direction.

Flemming and I continued across the carpet, through the kitchen and into the backyard. It was like an oasis back there, professionally landscaped and complete with a modest waterfall. It boasted an isolation that conflicted with the idea that it existed in a suburb.

"This is awesome," Flem commented.

"Yeah, it's pretty rad," Jess replied.

I loved it. Anything I do in my backyard is in full view of my neighbours in the suburb Alison and I live in.

"Come on, I'll show you my room," Jesse said.

Off to the side of the bungalow, Jesse's dimly-lit bedroom was instantly recognizable as that of a teenage music lover. The walls were barely visible in lieu of the rock posters that adorned them, clearly indicating that it was not a Demi Lovato fan who presided over the moody confines of this space. It felt the same as my teenage bedroom in terms of implied message, just a bit darker, maybe more sullen.

"Also pretty rad," I commented. I wished I could use the word *rad* with less responsibility.

"Yep, pretty rad."

A small period of silence prompted the three of us to look down to our shoes for inspiration.

"Well, I guess we should get going," were the words I chose with which to resume communication.

"Yeah," Flem chipped in. It was two-thirty in the afternoon, and we had to navigate Melbourne in search of a hotel room.

We said our kind-of-goodbyes to Jess inside the door, as we'd be seeing him a few hours later at Florida Discount Music. But the tour was over for him. He said he would be bringing his friends to FDM, along with the mothers of his friends. They all liked to go out to these types of things and have a few drinks.

Leaning against the van with arms folded, The Pink Chief awaited us under the hot Florida sun. My leather jacket would no longer be of any use to me now.

"Let's swing by my place, and then I'll set you guys up in a hotel close to the venue," he said.

"What's around there?" Flem asked. It was time to end our courtship with the Days Inn franchise.

"There's plenty. Sheratons, Hiltons, you name it."

We took our places in the van. As we backed out of the driveway, Jesse could not be seen through the window of his front door.

Down the road a few blocks from Florida Discount Music, Flemming turned in to the large parking lot of a Hilton Doubletree hotel. The Chief has led us here in his car after disembarking from the van at his house and removing his belongings. He had offered to take my books to the venue that night and set them up, as he'd be going early to liaise with his hometown crowd. Class act, The Pink Chief was. I was happy for him, as he would receive a king's welcome that night in his old stomping grounds. He deserved it. He had put a lot of effort into this thing.

Now, Flemming and I were on our own.

We checked in to the hotel and when we got up to our room on the 14th floor, we completed our load-in routine for the last time. The beer was put on ice in the sink, even though there was a refrigerator in the room. The bottles were still opened creatively. We chose to remain in character. It had seemed we'd been moving through this routine for much longer than a week, far away from the reality of the lives we had placed on hold back in Toronto. Now one last night remained.

Flemming propped himself up on his bed with a Samuel Adams as late afternoon sunshine flooded the room. He was watching whatever the sarcastically-named Learning Channel was offering. I was consumed with nervous energy. Should I try to get a quick nap in before the appearance? Start into the alcohol? Eat something? Couldn't decide. This week had been wearing me down a bit, doing funny things to my mind. Flemming probably sensed that I was mildly anxious.

"Want to grab some food downstairs?" he asked.

"Sure. After this beer?"

"Nah. Bring it with you."

I'm not big on that stuff. Open booze in public. I finished mine and placed the empty bottle on the desk. My frontal lobe responded accordingly.

"I'm good."

We walked out of the elevator and across the massive lobby to the restaurant on the other side. "Table for two, please," said my dinner date with a huge smile, in his usual plucky tone. Steve Flemming, human Xanax.

We sat down and Flem rested his can of warmish beer on the table, reclining in his chair. A colder replacement was placed in front of him, with mine arriving shortly after. The clock on the restaurant wall was counting out my seconds for me now.

"Let's get drunk and talk about classic Canadian musicians," I urged.

"How classic are we talking?" Flem replied.

"Harlequin, Streetheart, Max Webster. Loverboy. Headpins," I responded. "And Prism. Ron Tabak from Prism was very mildly reminiscent of Axl Rose on *Armageddon*. You can hear shades of Axl if you listen closely to his singing."

"Dude. I've never even *heard* of Prism."

"And you call yourself a Canadian?"

"When did *Armageddon* come out?"

"Around 1979," I said.

I did the math in my head. I got the record for Christmas when I was about ten, so it had to be 1979.

"Did this Tarrack guy sound like the singer from Nazareth?"

"*Tabak*. And no. Not at all."

I knew Nazareth's Dan McCafferty was an Axl Rose influence, but I never really acknowledged any vocal similarities between the two. I doubt Tabak had influenced Rose at all, but who knows? Lars Ulrich used to listen to Winnipeg band Streetheart back in the day. Hell, so did Ace Frehley – his solo band Frehley's Comet covered a Streetheart song in 1988 on their *Second Sighting* record. And Neil Schon's side project Hardline had a minor hit in 1992 with Streetheart-penned "Hot Cherie". As little known as they may have been, Streetheart, like Prism, was a great band. It seemed like that same greatness was shared among all of those bands back then, though some of them are possibly held in a more adulated regard based on their vintage. We do this all the time. Sometimes things can be better as memories than they are as actual things.

"Is Prism still around?" Flem asked, feigning interest. He was more interested in the fish tacos he had ordered from our waitress Donna. Flem wasn't interested in Donna – she looked to be in her mid-sixties. Nice lady though.

"No" I said. "Tabak died in a weird accident in the early eighties."

Tabak had been fired from the band before the accident and Prism carried on without him, but Ron Tabak *was* Prism in my mind. His voice was incredible.

Flem became a bit more interested in the conversation after the mention of a *weird accident*. He looked up at me.

"What happened?"

"Tabak had been invited by Prism's guitar player Al Harlow to spend Christmas with him at his home. For some unknown reason, Tabak decided to ride his bicycle over to Harlow's house. No helmet, no lights. Turned out to be a bad idea, because it was nighttime and the roads were covered in snow and ice."

"Yeah," Flem muttered. For the moment I was prevailing over the fish taco that was releasing a discreet vapour up towards his face as it sat in front of him.

"The story goes that Tabak was struck by a passing vehicle and that he fell off his bike and hit his head. He was brought to the hospital by ambulance. He seemed fine, and the doctor didn't find anything wrong with him. So they sent him on his way. They released him."

"Yeah?" Flem's acknowledgement took on the intonation of a question as he leaned in closer.

"Then, all of a sudden, Tabak started getting abusive." My inflection began to lend itself to a campfire horror story tone. "Abusive to the point where police officers at the hospital had to restrain him and place him under arrest."

"Then what?"

The taco didn't stand a chance at this point.

"The cops thought he was loaded, and so they threw him in the drunk tank."

"And did he get killed in there?"

"No. He was found unconscious in his cell and they rushed him back to the hospital. When they re-examined him, they found a huge blood clot on the right side of his brain. He passed away before they could operate. He died on Christmas Day, 1984."

"Wow. That's crazy." Flemming said quietly.

"Isn't it?"

Flem focused on the wood grain of the table for a moment. Then, a goofy smile crossed his face as he looked up at me.

"Maybe Axl Rose is Ron Tabak reincarnated."

"Eat your taco, you fucking clown," I responded.

༄

One or two more drinks back in our room at the hotel to toast this upcoming night of revelry, in what would be the crescendo of our haphazard trek across the southeastern United States of America. We both knew this night would be the highlight of this tour. We were amped up for it.

Tonight our event would be hosted by local rock impresario Charles Knight, a respected veteran of the Melbourne music scene who had played in bands on LA's Sunset Strip in the eighties. He'd read my book and had been following our exploits over this past week on Facebook, and he messaged me suggesting an after-party jam with his band at another Melbourne bar. Perfect. I was looking forward to meeting him and everyone else who would be there. Being in the cab on the way to

Florida Discount Music felt like being drawn back in the pouch of a slingshot, gradually further and further, until being catapulted at full speed into the nighttime.

When Flemming and I walked into FDM just before seven, a sizeable crowd had already gathered. We made our way toward the group through the music store portion of the premises. The walls were adorned with Dean, ESP, and Taylor guitars, the floors lined with amplifiers of all sorts. Towards the back of the store was an expansive area called Open Mike's, which featured a stage on the right, a bar on the left, and tables and chairs in between. People of all age and stripe mingled and drank in this space as we approached. There were young girls with their youngish-looking mothers. Black men wearing patterned sweaters and cowboy hats. Waiflike longhaired metalhead kids wearing black skinny jeans and t-shirts that hung from their collarbones. Women dressed in leopard-print bodysuits and spike heels with hair reminiscent of Jenilee Harrison. Plunging necklines and optimized cleavage as far as the eye could see. Hair, leather jackets, and denim were the order of the day. I scanned the room from one side to the other and back again, nodding my head in silent approval. This was going to be an extremely fun group.

Curious eyes moved over Flemming and me as we penetrated this congregation. A guy with a serious camera was circling the crowd, inconspicuously snapping photographic documentation of the event. It's a funny feeling, being in that position. Kinda like posing for a really long picture. My recurring intrigue with the constructs of fame and how easily and deceptively it can be manufactured was piqued.

I'd read about people who had fashioned themselves as highly successful entrepreneurs in their online social media profiles, but ended up in fact committing suicide because their lives were so painfully opposite to their fabricated online personae.

These are extreme cases, but I think about this stuff when I use Twitter and Facebook. I used to be a bit more obnoxious in posting messages as a means of generating some attention towards *No Sleep 'Til Sudbury*, as this was the point – I wouldn't have a Twitter account unless I had something to promote. The reality is that at its core, Twitter is a promotional vehicle. But I reconsidered my approach after meeting people associated with the book and interacting with them, because I'm nothing like my Twitter profile in real life. I couldn't continue posting this way in good conscience, as I felt a bit like the man behind the curtain in some respects. But maybe no one paid attention to that. Or maybe it's expected. Either way, the illusion of fame is easily crafted. I've always been very intrigued by the basic concept of it.

Charles Knight eventually appeared in front of me, flashing a meaningful smile. He stood out in a crowd. His mane of sun-bleached hair fell straight and long beyond the collar of his white button-down shirt. He looked like a warm, rugged cross between Rutger Hauer and David Coverdale, imbued with a no-nonsense vibe that earned him the distinction of being recognized as the de facto leader of this tribe. The lines in his face invited me to consider the many rock and roll stories I hoped he would share with me at some point during my time here. I sensed that his respect would have to be earned. I liked that. We shook hands.

"How are you, man?" Charles asked.

"Been good, dude. Happy to be here."

We'd been communicating briefly on Facebook over the course of our travels, but I almost felt like I knew Charles already.

"It's great to have you here," he said.

We talked a bit about the event and the post-event jam festivities, and I was stoked. Charles then introduced his girlfriend Lissa. Her smile lit up the place. She was the queen of this scene; friendly, vibrant, dressed to stun and then kill. It was clear that the girl knew how to enjoy herself. She and Charles made me feel very much at ease, and I looked forward to the night's possibilities with these folks as my Floridian hosts.

Chris Long, as he was known here, was being revered by several well-wishers in another corner of the room. He truly was The Pink Chief now, holding court with his pink beret set back on his head, bright blue button-down shirt with sleeves rolled up to reveal bracelets galore, and with trademark pink Hannah Montana bag in tow. He was being celebrated here by people who genuinely loved him. It was a fulfilling scene. Hometown kid made good. After a few minutes, I made my way over and he introduced me to each of his supporters. Nice people.

"Well my man, what do you say? You ready to rock this thing?" he asked in his Nicholsonian drawl. I looked around the room. It was well after seven o'clock and the space was now full.

"Ready when you are, sir." I spied Flemming over his shoulder, chatting at the bar toward the back of this place. He made eye contact, lifted his pint glass, and raised his eyebrows as he nodded in the direction of the signing table set up on the stage. I turned to look, and saw a full pint sitting beside the pile of *No Sleep 'Til Sudbury* copies The Chief had kindly already assembled on the table. I looked back at him, smiling and shaking my head in appreciation. He winked and turned away, continuing his conversation.

"Alright, let's do this."

After some last-minute milling about we took our places beside each other at the table, positioning our mics and shifting our props around anxiously in front of the crowd that had assembled. Chief set up his laptop. Charles was set up over to our left on the stage, also with a microphone and a laptop containing the written introduction with which he would address our guests to kick off the proceedings. He was fully prepared.

This guy continued to impress me. In his intro speech, Charles provided his interpretation of our books, and looked the audience (and us) directly in the eye while delivering it. His perspective was thoughtful and even-keeled, and I was happy that he found *No Sleep* so enjoyable, if not overly *analytical* – he stressed this word as he spoke it, turning to nod in my direction, looking at me with furled brow but with a smile. Dude was legitimate. There was no bullshit.

Following his introduction, Charles asked if we'd like to do a reading from our books. The Chief complied, reading a snippet from his laptop. I don't recall if it was the same one he had read in Macon, mostly because I had been taking the time to look over the crowd while Chief basked in his limelight. My eyes rested on a chap sitting at a table just off the stage right in front of me. He wore a black leather jacket, as did the blonde in thigh-high boots with whom he shared the table. His brown hair was slightly shorter than it was in my memory, but he still looked much the same as he did when I saw his photograph all those years ago. For a few seconds my mind worked to affix a name to the subject of this photo. Ah yes, I remembered – Jack Starr, guitarist from Virgin Steele. Wow. There he was.

Virgin Steele had helped pioneer the burgeoning early 80s American power metal scene that would eventually spawn bands like Metallica. I used to listen to Virgin Steele in my bedroom as a kid back then, and now the guy who cranked out those riffs was seated right here in front of me. I contemplated the mind-bending distance between then and where we currently found ourselves.

As The Chief concluded the reading of his passage, he turned things over to me. Even though this crowd was fully engaged and a reading would have been welcomed, I still didn't feel like I wanted to go that route. I elected to talk to the crowd about the book's ethos and why I wrote it instead. The conversation eventually worked its way around to my reiterating the Gene Simmons story, based on the fact that the radio interview from earlier in the day had been heard by most of the audience. From here, Charles morphed the proceedings into a question and answer period.

Multiple hands were raised simultaneously. There were plenty of questions, all thoughtful and interesting. This was a great crowd. Every face in the audience bore an engaged expression, with the exception of two gentlemen sitting on raised barstools to the left of the room. Their faces were skeptical as they nursed their Bud Lights; they gave the impression of a boyfriend who was having to sit through the chick flick, far enough into the relationship that he didn't care if his facial expression betrayed his position. When I answered the next couple of questions I turned in their direction to make eye contact with them, nodding and smiling as I spoke. I tried to bring them in. This moved the needle very little, however. I wondered why these guys were there. Maybe melancholy was their happiness, as it was for the guys in Slipknot. Maybe their scowling denoted the fact that they were in fact thrilled to be there. They likely didn't realize they were being perceived by me in this way. Didn't matter a whole lot, really. I was actually more concerned with preparing myself for the possibility of Bobby Dall bursting into the room and swinging one of his basses in the direction of The Pink Chief's head.

When someone in the crowd asked me about the bands I listened to as a kid, I made a point of incorporating Jack into the discussion by including Virgin Steele into my answer and gesturing in his direction. He nodded and smiled in appreciation. He seemed like a grounded, humble individual. I was stoked that he was there, and I looked forward to chatting with him afterwards.

The gap between questions was increasing now, signaling that the Q&A period was coming to an end. I saw a single hand go up in my periphery. My eyes shifted to the left and locked in with those of my questioner, barely visible under the brim of his black ball cap. It was one of the scowlers.

"Yeah - guy with the glare?" I didn't really say that. Out loud anyway. I anticipated heckling, or at least a difficult question.

"Two questions," he intoned.

"Shoot," I responded.

"How long did it take you to write the book?"

This wasn't so bad. I'd answered this question a million times already, into a mic and in personal conversation, even though I wasn't entirely sure of the precise answer.

"I'd say it took me probably two and a half to three years in total. It started out as a bunch of articles I'd written for webzines, but then I figured I could compile them all into a book by weaving them together with a common theme. That theme would be what it was like to experience this music as a teenager growing up in a small, isolated town in the 80s. So I sequestered myself in a room with the door closed every Saturday from noon until around five, and just wrote. I couldn't write every day because I have a full-time career, and I didn't want to do nothing but write on the weekends because then it would have seemed like work. So that went on for between two and a half to three years. My wife thought I was nuts at first, but she eventually came around."

Couple of snickers in the crowd. No change in facial expression from my questioner. What would his second question be?

"Okay. Next question," he replied. I leaned in.

"Do you have a proper working visa to be down here selling these books?"

The straight face he tried to keep after asking this question gave way to a smile. The crowd laughed.

"I do" I answered, "as far as you know."

⤳

After the Q&A period wrapped up, the audience formed a line and The Pink Chief and I began to put Sharpie to book and posed for pictures with our new friends. Most of these people were in fact Chief's old friends, and loyal ones at that.

"Pleased to meet you," one man said. "Any friend of Christopher's is a friend of mine."

This is a powerful statement to make when it's genuine, which it was. This was not lost on me; it was an example of the distinct sense of community I picked up on since Flem and I had arrived. I got the impression that these people all depended on each other to some meaningful extent. And Jack Starr was a proud member of this group.

"I'm really looking forward to reading this book, Brent" he said, approaching me with hand outstretched.

"I'm glad to hear that, Jack. I hope you like it," I replied as I shook his picking hand.

Over the course of our chat about Virgin Steele and his current band Burning Starr, he gave me a copy of their latest CD, *Land of the Dead*. As I signed his copy of *No Sleep 'Til Sudbury*, he personalized the disc's jacket for me. It was a gratifying moment for a small town metal kid who used to listen to this guy from the other end of the stereo.

"Y'know" Jack said pensively, "had this album been released in 1986 it would be a huge hit."

I didn't doubt this at all. In fact, I began to feel as though it *was* 1986 during this evening, as if I had somehow slipped through a hole in the fabric of the space-time continuum. I knew that most people in the room felt the same way, and that this was their specific intention. It felt remarkably easy to float along through this manufactured wrinkle in time. The past was the present, and nothing else mattered. The ease in my reversion was directly influenced by this assembled group of the rock and roll faithful, embodied by Jack Starr himself.

"Maybe you'd be interested in writing my biography for your next project," he said with a sly smile. "We could call it *The Boy Who Didn't Get His Ice Cream*. Ritchie Blackmore referred to me in this way in the past."

Fascinating. It would take some time for me to digest this. I wasn't sure how serious he was, if at all. He was likely kidding. I thought a lot about the documentary possibilities. Still do. I would think a lot about Jack in general over the days that followed, and his steadfast devotion to his music. I was glad to have met him.

The Pink Chief stood beside me after Jack and I finished our conversation. "Hey, we need to make sure we swap books before this is all over," he said.

"Definitely" I responded.

"And I want mine autographed," Chief smiled.

"You got it, man."

After the last folks in the room had their books signed, Chief pulled one more copy of *C'MON!* from a box behind him and looked at me with an impish grin. I opened up a copy of my book to the third page and wrote a personalized message to him on it, closed the book and slid it across the table to him. Our time together was drawing to a close.

My quirky co-pilot looked up at me as I watched him form block letters with the pink Sharpie he had been using all night. He anticipated a smartass comment from me, but none came. I smiled at him. He finished writing, blew on the fuchsia ink, and pushed the closed copy over to me. I opened it up again to read his inscription:

To Brent:

Simply put,
I love you!

Chris
2013

Below this, in quotes towards the corner of the page, he had written a line that made me laugh out loud. It was perfect:

"Come on in!"

Fourteen
Bang a Gong

~

"Well, you ready? It's party time, brothers!"

Charles Knight, event moderator would now morph into the role of Charles Knight, rock star.

"Welcome to Steagle's!"

I hunched down in the passenger seat, lowering my head slightly to look up at the bar's entrance through the window of Lissa's car as it came to a stop. The corners of my mouth curled up into a smile. Everybody out.

"Where are your books?" Charles asked.

"I left them with Chris."

The Chief was good enough to hang onto the remainder of unsold books I was left with now that the appearances had concluded. He didn't come along to Steagle's, despite my leaning on him heavily to do so during our goodbyes. But I understood.

"You gotta get them back! We're gonna sell them here tonight!" Charles responded vehemently.

"Really?" I said, surprised.

"Yeah, *really!*"

Damn. Should I call The Chief to bother him for the books? Poor guy. He's probably trying to chill out after his big night. Maybe he wouldn't care though. Would he? The guy's golden. He'd be fine with driving them over. *Yeah.* My fingers fumbled over the keypad of my iPhone.

"Hello?" He sounded drowsy.

"Hey!" I greeted him. "Charlie says I should try to sell off the rest of my books here. Would it be okay to ask if you could drive them over? We're at Steagle's." I didn't even know how far away he lived. He was likely nonplussed. I hate dealing with drunks when I haven't been drinking. As a teetotaler, I can just imagine how he felt about getting this call.

"Of course," came that Nicholson thing. "Be right over."

"He's coming!" I exclaimed, maybe a bit too excitedly. I was surprised he answered. Maybe he didn't have call display. I shouldn't have called, I regretted it.

A short time later with the box of books in tow Flemming, Lissa, Charlie, and I walked into the bar. An assemblage of musicians was in mid-song on a large stage to our left. I could feel the low end pulsing through my shins. I don't remember what song they were playing. Charlie slung an arm across my shoulders.

"The list of people who call me Charlie is a very, very short one, just so you know" he said in my ear, with equal parts menace and sincerity. Lissa overheard this and smiled in our direction.

"I get that" I responded, "and I have an appreciation for the distinction."

Charlie smiled.

I stood back to take in my surroundings. Steagle's Pub was a dirty rock and roll roadhouse - worn in, loose, and easy, the way the best rock bars are. Tables and chairs were strewn across the middle of the room, which was gradually becoming the dance floor as the booze flowed and the crowd proliferated. Neon beer signs glowed like insignias of promise for what I assumed were loyal patrons who took their regular positions throughout this place. I felt like they all came here to relinquish their troubles, to alleviate the pain that can come with being an adult.

The band ended their song with a loud syncopated crash. A maniacal expression washed over Charlie's face as the cymbals completed their decay. He grabbed one of the books from the box and leapt up onto the stage with wild eyes.

"*What's up, people??!*" he shouted into the microphone. The crowd cheered their approval. I felt a chill run through my rib cage.

"We have a friend of mine here with us tonight," Charlie continued. "His name is Brent Jensen, and he wrote this book, it's called *No Sleep 'Til Sudbury!*"

Christ. I was overwhelmed by this. Wasn't expecting it at all.

"There he is right there!" Charlie pointed me out at the back of the place, then raised his hand with fingers spread and began waving.

"Say hi to Brent, everyone!"

Most of the crowd turned around to face me.

"Hi Brent!" their voices yelled in unison, waving and smiling.

I raised my hand and waved back, humbled. "Hello everybody!" I shouted. Flemming was laughing his drunken ass off.

"Now listen. Brent has copies of his book here, and I want you to buy a copy from him, okay?" Charlie continued, nodding in the affirmative. Some members of the clergy nodded back. This place belonged to him.

"Okay, great. Thank you!" Charlie spoke into the mic and winked at me.

"*Now do you want to hear some rock and roll?*" he screamed. The crowd roared, and the band stormed into Zeppelin's "Rock and Roll".

It couldn't have been any more perfect, really.

⌒○

"That can't be right," I said.

I could have said this about a number of things I had experienced this past week, including the assertion that the bartender in Steagle's was no longer a teenager. I could have sworn she still was. However, at this moment I was referring to the cost of the four beers Flem had just ordered from this young lady.

"It *is* right – *two dollars*. That's what she said." The volume of Flem's voice was competing with the band's rendition of Motley Crue's "Live Wire".

I looked at the small, skinny blonde girl behind the bar for affirmation. She looked back at me and shrugged, raising her eyebrows and shoulders simultaneously.

Fifty cent beers. I still wasn't convinced. Flemming was, though. And he was motivated. He was buying trays of them and passing them out to all of his new Steagle's friends. Later on he would be behind the bar pouring beers and mixing drinks. The kid had a gift, and he was definitely in his element here. Time to board up the windows. Hurricane Flemming was approaching the Florida coastline.

The band finished their set. It appeared the guitar player was the only constant among the musical flotsam and jetsam responsible for the tunes. I drank from one of the glasses from Flem's tray as I stood and watched this crew of musos tend to their instruments while everyone else turned away, headed for the tiny bathrooms. I felt a hand on my shoulder.

"Hey, when do you want to go up?" It was Charlie.

"Ready anytime. What's the drill?"

The guitar player appeared. We shook hands and exchanged names. His name was Troy.

"What do you want to sing?" Troy asked.

"Do you know any Guns N' Roses?"

"Nah, I don't play that stuff," he dismissed with a scowl.

"Um, I don't know. Wanna do "Roadhouse Blues"?" I figured it was a good fit for this bar, this crowd. Troy shook his head.

"Nope."

"STP?" I was a bit reluctant to make any more suggestions.

"How about AC/DC?" Troy countered.

Ah, yes. AC/DC was good.

"Sin City?" I asked.

"Uh, I don't know about that one. The timing of those chords at the beginning and the end might be tough to line up with the bass player. I don't know if he's done that one before."

We went back and forth on the possibilities for a while as we finished our drinks. It would be "Sin City" after all, right after the break concluded.

When you're drinking and playing, not having to worry about the guitar is a huge plus. Just singing is preferred to singing and playing guitar at the same time in these situations. I tend to focus more on one of them over the other after a few, often with disastrous results. "Sin City" was a song that I'd sang and played guitar on in live situations before, but on this night I was happy to leave the guitar duties to someone else.

The break was over. Now it was time once again to enter the wonderful world of rock and roll make-believe.

As it always did, the left hand reached up and curled around the microphone, as the right hand found the mic stand just above the height adjustment clutch. Both hands tightened their grip for just a moment to commemorate a special union, this manipulation familiar and a little bit magical each and every time. The shoulders dropped with neck stretched outward toward the crowd, eyes surveying the collection of bodies. During this assessment, the right hand guides the mic stand clutch inward once or twice allowing the microphone to be lifted up to within inches of the lips, and then worked again in the opposite direction to lock the length of the stand in place. All set.

A nod to the timekeeper behind us. Now, his drumsticks could be heard clicking together to count out time, almost serving as a warning.

Thick, bludgeoning chords exploded from the speakers, lent additional power by the thumping bass and cymbals with kick-drum accompaniment. Multi-coloured lights washed over the stage. The left hand remained on the mic while the right side of the body opened up, the right hand free to convey all of those sensations so eagerly absorbed from long ago rock posters scotch-taped to adolescent bedroom walls. The rhythm guided the bodies in the crowd along in unison, as if they were entranced marionettes under its sway. The 747 was taking off again. And I was wearing the pilot's uniform.

The sound in the room was great again here in Melbourne. The floor monitors before my feet projected my voice back up to me with crystal clarity and perfect volume. The words flowed from my mouth as time seemed to just freeze, allowing my mind to evaluate the momentous beauty of this elusive reality.

The bass crept along independently in the song's breakdown, encouraging a swirling sociopathy behind my eyes while I described ladders and snakes, beggars and thieves in lowered register. All together, we braced for the impact of those big bashing chords that would return for the song's crescendo. I squeezed the mic stand in my fists as they sounded with so much authority, swaying back and forth on spread legs.

Bang!

Bang!

Bang!

Bang!

During the last bridge, across that chugging A chord that ascends to a D, I spat the lyric lines into the microphone in anticipation of that last chorus. The music was fluidity that surrounded me with a freedom I know I could never hold on to, the freedom that breaks my heart just a little bit every time it leaves me. That moment was coming now. I turned to face the drummer and with my back to the crowd, I lifted the mic stand up over my head in front of the drummer to mark the unleashing of the song's final pummeling chords:

E – A – B – D – A – B....EEEEEEEEEEEEEEEEEEEEEEEEEE

As that last E chord rang out, thick curtains of emotion poured forth. This was glory. Purest bliss. All of it coming from the most honest of places.

The song ended with a final thundering crash now:

BAAAANG!

Providence.

Over the din of the crowd, I turned to Troy and reached out to shake his hand. He had sounded great, as did the whole band.

"Nice fucking job, man!" I yelled in his ear.

Lissa jumped up on stage and grabbed a mic.

"You wanna do another one?"

The crowd began shouting out requests. We abruptly decided to stay with AC/DC, doing an alternate verse duet of "Dirty Deeds Done Dirt Cheap". There was no telling how it would go, but this was all part of the fun – no one in this place cared. Everyone just wanted to enjoy themselves and let loose.

Singing the same verse twice and forgetting the words were directly attributed to those fifty cent beers that Flemming continued to hand out. No matter. Lissa and I laughed our way through to the choruses, singing the *dirty deeds* part and then holding our mics outward to the crowd for their contribution. The band remained solid. Applause and much love all around after we finished. This place was great, and Lissa and Charlie had been incredible hosts.

⌒◯

As the night continued to unfold inside Steagle's Pub, I moved around the place and grew more familiar with its patrons. Together we would engage in all manner of discussion – lots of musical dialogue, some storytelling, some local lore, skill-testing questions about Canadian geography, and more. At one point I found myself at the back of the establishment, having discovered an exit onto a crude patio-smoking-area-type hangout where some folks had gathered to partake of the nicotine.

I used to smoke when I drank. More than a pack a night at the height of it. I only ever smoked when I drank. Didn't care for it at all at any other time. I felt like smoking lined up nicely with whatever resistance I was propagating back when we were smoother and stronger. It felt foreign to *not* have a lit cigarette between the index and middle finger of my right hand when the drink was flowing in those days, years ago.

And now, on this most glorious of evenings, one where drinking and rock and roll were of prime essence, a pack of Marlboro Lights would have been a perfect accoutrement. If I was ever going to get back into the smoking, this would have been the night. But...I just didn't *want* one. Even in my inebriation, reason was consistently informing my judgment as I grew older. This isn't so much a precursor to wisdom as it is an ever-increasing awareness of mortality. As I age these things loom larger in the mind – heart attack, stroke, cancer, and how impossible it seems that Keith Richards has managed to elude each of these harbingers of death despite his being, well...*Keef.* I really do need to think more like Keef. I'm wound up too tight most of the time. When I drive on the highway, I imagine the plausibility of that cigarette butt thrown out the window by the guy in front of me being able to somehow bounce up under my car and ignite my gas tank, blowing me up. I think about shit like that all the time. I never used to think like that when I was smoking a pack a night. Now I'm inventing multiple ways by which cigarettes can do me in. I blame advanced age for this. And the Internet.

Screw all of that mortality consideration. Tonight in Steagle's, it was time for some uplifting and enlightening discourse.

"There aren't enough gongs in rock songs anymore," I offered to this smallish group of smoking rockers as we subconsciously formed a circle. I believed that none of these people were younger than me.

My postulation was legitimate. The gong, just as the Japanese rising sun and the pentagram were to 80s metal, served as important rock symbolism during the late 70s and early 80s. John Bonham, Alex Van Halen, and loads of other drummers employed the gong as an essential fixture behind their drum kits back then. Nobody did this anymore in post-rock and roll America or anywhere else (except maybe Japan). These are things I think about when I'm not wondering how cigarettes are going to kill me.

"How many songs *did* have gongs in them?" came the question from one of the faithful who saw the potential for an interesting exchange.

I knew of four songs with gongs in them right off the top of my head. These songs were "Bohemian Rhapsody" by Queen, "I Don't Know" by Ozzy Osbourne, Aerosmith's "Dream On", and "Almost Human" by KISS. I could likely come up with five or six more if I went away and really thought about it.

"There has to be at least twenty or thirty," someone blurted out. That seemed aggressive. I couldn't name half that many.

"I'd say there are probably ten that we could name right now," I responded. I was careful with my tone. I was a guest here.

"Does the live version of "Unchained" by Van Halen count?" one of the guys said. It did not, in my opinion. The gong had to appear in the studio version of the song for it to count.

"You getting that from the video?" I asked. That's where I had seen it, Alex Van Halen having the lit the exterior ring of the gong on fire, and then thrashing away at it with a large mallet to conclude the live rendering of the song.

"Yeah," he nodded.

"Doesn't count," I said.

"Why not?"

"Because it's not the original studio version of the song," I replied. *Tone.*

"He's right," someone else contributed. "If Roth played a purple kazoo during the live version of "Unchained", we couldn't say that the kazoo was a significant instrumental contribution to the actual song."

Right. Interesting use of a modifier, but I think I understood where this guy was going with that.

"Lots of things can happen during a live show, lots of variation from an instrumental standpoint, right?" I was looking for examples in my mind, as I figured I would be called out on this. "These interpretations should be considered as being separate from the actual *song* itself, because it's just a version of something that's already been established," I continued.

"Like what?"

There. Called out. Knew it.

"Like, uh..." I stammered.

All eyes stared into my face.

"Like when Scott Weiland sings songs through a megaphone live that weren't sung through a megaphone during their original recording."

Whew.

"Guns songs, you mean?"

"Guns N' Roses songs, STP songs, Velvet Revolver songs. Whatever."

"But those would technically be covers, right? Would that count?" This question came from one of the members of our group who had previously been silent. He was biding his time. He seemed proud of this interjection.

"Different kettle of fish altogether," I answered. "But if Scott Weiland sang an original Stone Temple Pilots song live with the Stone Temple Pilots band using a megaphone, as he did on "Crackerman", this would be the example I would use."

I wasn't certain whether or not it was a megaphone Weiland used on the studio version of "Crackerman". And with any luck, no one would challenge the grounds on which a megaphone could be considered a musical instrument.

"What about the fucking gong examples?" one of the guys yelled out. Booze had usurped any requirement for courtesy in this discourse, as it typically did.

"Right" I said. "Ozzy Osbourne, "I Don't Know". Right at the beginning of the song."

"Yes!"

Lots of reminiscent smiles and nodding. This was likely in addition to much mental conjuring of the guitarist who made that song so incredible, the late great Randy Rhoads.

"Randy fucking *rocked*," someone pitched in. I agreed. He was one of my all-time faves.

"And "Bohemian Rhapsody", right at the end," the formerly silent guy said. This would have been easier had we all introduced ourselves. But that may have seemed unusual in this setting.

I still had two gong songs in my hat, but I was careful. I didn't want to seem like a smug prick. I waited for someone to fire out the Aerosmith example. A few of these guys had to know the KISS example. The gong is so blatant in that song that it almost scares you.

"Did "Get It On (Bang a Gong)" have a gong in it?" someone asked, not surprisingly. I didn't know if the T. Rex version did, and it didn't matter if the Power Station version did.

The comment was dismissed as the silent chap interjected.

"Zeppelin uses a gong, I think, but I don't know which song they use it in. Could be a couple." This guy wasn't silent anymore at all. Now he was the most verbose fella in this bunch.

While this exchange continued, part of my brain was off somewhere else, shuffling through rock tunes searching for the presence of gongs in songs I knew. There had to be a gong somewhere on the *Use Your Illusion* records – every other instrument known to man seems to appear on those albums. And Bowie had to have used a gong at some point. I recalled that (one of) the Led Zeppelin songs this guy mentioned was in fact "What Is and What Should Never Be". We used to play this song in an old band, and the drummer would try to replicate the subdued gong sound with his china cymbal, with very little success.

"Sweet Leaf!" someone yelled out.

Mother*fucker*...! He was right. Completely missed that one. The gong sounds three times during the pickup in the middle of that old Sabbath chestnut. It's loud and aggressive, too - probably Ozzy bashing away at it, all boozed up. Of *course* Black Sabbath would have used a gong. I wondered if there had been a gong on Sabbath's excellent *Sabotage* record. There had to be. If there wasn't, there should have been.

Fellow countrymen Rush also had to have employed a gong during their early *flowing robes* period. I wasn't so familiar with that material, so I put it out there.

"How about Rush? Any gong tunes from the early records?" I asked.

"Maybe "Hemispheres" has one?" someone asked in return.

I shrugged. "Not sure."

Most of this group stared so intensely at the floor it was as if they were trying to pull gong song examples out of it with their eyes.

And then it came. *"Ah!* "Dream On"! Right at the end before those two repeating notes fade out!" We had a winner.

It occurred to me at that moment that Queensryche also used a gong on their *Rage For Order* record, at the end of "Gonna Get Close To You". Maybe. Or maybe it was another song. Whatever the song was, the gong was heard right at the very end. I couldn't place it. Curse Flemming's fifty cent beer tray for making this more difficult than it had to be. The way he was throwing those beers around, his new nickname should have been Fitty Cent in place of Crystal the next day.

"Does Toto's "Africa" count?" one of the guys said with a smile. It did at this point.

Wait. That was it. It was "The Whisper" by Queensryche, the song right before "Gonna Get Close To You" on *Rage For Order*! I decided to hold this one back. I would have felt like Jim Parsons' Sheldon character from *The Big Bang Theory* putting that one out there.

"I got a fever, and the only prescription is more *gong*!" the newly verbose chap laughed. He cracked himself up. He was the life of the party now. Party Boy.

As such, I elected not to go down the road I had thought this dialogue likely would – how the fact that the gong's absence could be paralleled with the absence of a certain artistry from rock, and that this could ultimately be represented as a signifier of rock's demise, lending credence to the premise that rock and roll was in fact - *dead.* Or had at least degenerated to the point where it was being only replicated now as retro novelty. The invention and creativity had been exhausted.

But there was no need to illuminate such a potentially morose fact in this currently cheerful setting. No need for a descent into negativity. Best to keep the merriment and the fifty cent beer flowing freely. This was a night for celebration.

"KISS used the gong at least once that I can remember," I offered. "On "Almost Human" from the *Love Gun* record."

"Yeah!" Party Boy screamed, bolting from his chair. "That's right!" He broke into the song's chorus. *"I'm almost a ma-a-aan!"*

Party Boy was right. We almost were.

Fifteen

Doro & The God of Thunder

~

Sometime after midnight Flemming and I left Steagle's Pub with Charlie, Lissa, and some of their friends to embark on a tour of some other Melbourne establishments. Along the way we arrived at a bar that was nearly empty, a place that may or may not have been called Lou's Blues. Upon entering I looked up to see a large stage looming thirty feet above our heads, open to the floor below and accessible only from the second level. Red and yellow neon signs advertised local beer and augmented the dim purple lighting. Cool place.

As we stood around the bar beneath the stage drinking and chatting, a chap who looked to be in his early twenties suddenly appeared out of nowhere. He took everyone by surprise, and he was visibly intoxicated. For a minute or so, he just stood there silently and without expression, looking at all of us, eyes dim. Charlie and one of his friends closed in toward him with slow, deliberate Clint Eastwood menace. The tension was percolating just a little bit.

"What's up, man?" I said to him. I didn't want this guy to get his ass kicked, but truth be told I didn't really have a lot of patience for weird stuff like this either. We didn't know what his intentions were.

"Who is...this...book?" he said in a thick accent. Not great with the English language, or monumentally hammered. Or both. He would have to speak again before I could place the accent. He looked European; Nordic features with blue eyes and sandy hair. Young. Kinda like the *before* version of Thor. He was pointing to a copy of *No Sleep 'Til Sudbury* that one of Charlie's friends, a guy named Tommy, was holding in his hand. I had just signed the cover of this copy for him a minute ago as we stood at the bar. I don't typically sign the cover, but when I had opened the book to the third page to sign where I usually did, Tommy requested the cover be signed instead. Unusual, but it actually looked pretty cool.

"I'm sorry?" I asked.

"Are you the book....?" he trailed off.

"Author?"

"Yes, right," he nodded enthusiastically.

Turned out dude *was* both – Scandinavian sounding and challenged by the English language, and also very buzzed. He reeked of liquor.

"What kind of music? Like, Metallica?" he mumbled. Tensions eased in the group now.

"Yeah. Metallica, KISS, Guns N' Roses. No Poison though," I said.

Then, a woman appeared from behind him.

"You know Scorpions?" she questioned, in the same accent Skinny Thor spoke in.

"Yeah, I know Scorpions. I don't *know* them, but I've heard of them. They're in the book," I responded.

"I *know* them," she spat back. Maybe she was German. In the haze, I couldn't say for sure. She reminded me of Doro Pesch from 80s Viking-metal band Warlock - long blond hair, high cheekbones. Early to mid-twenties. Looked like she could have been a performer. She was an attractive girl, and she definitely knew it. Her face defaulted to a puckery pout when she wasn't making a sassy one.

"She is well-known singer in Europe. She play festival," Skinny Thor slurred.

"Is she your girlfriend?" someone asked. This question was irrelevant.

"No. We are just friends."

184

Over the bar's system, GN'R's "You Could Be Mine" was playing. Doro pointed up to the ceiling. "I sing all Guns N' Roses, better than Axl," she sneered.

Good lord. She said her name, but we were too far along for me to remember what it was. I do remember that it didn't mean anything to me when I heard it. She was very insistent and standoffish, like she was trying to establish some point other than her intended one - that she was a famous singer. I felt like this may have been a fib, at the very least an exaggeration.

She reminded me of this Serbian guy who was a pathological liar I used to live with in dorm back in university. He used to tell us that he was on the Serbian Olympic diving team and shit like that. And he was *adamant* about it. He wouldn't let up. Dude had a body like a milk bag; there was no way he had recently represented any country in Olympic diving, or in any other competition that was remotely athletic. The day he moved in to dorm he tried cooking Kraft Dinner by pouring the powder packet into the boiling water while the noodles were still cooking. Then while all of his roommates laughed at him, he tried to recover by telling us this was the proper way of preparing Kraft Dinner where he was from. This behaviour continued for the duration of the school year. Fucking joker.

So, as I did back in dorm, I figured the next logical step would be to confirm this initial information we'd been provided with by Doro. If she was in fact a famous singer who commanded festival-sized crowds, surely it wouldn't be unreasonable to request a sampling of her talent for the purposes of validation.

"You can sing Guns songs better than Axl?" I asked. "Go ahead, sing along with this one. C'mon. Just a few lines." Over the system, Axl was coming into the last chorus of "You Could Be Mine".

She looked skyward as if the band was actually playing somewhere up there.

"No, I won't. I am not monkey," she said, smiling with a condescension that was entirely intended. Her eyes were intense, searing a hole into my face.

"I didn't say you were a monkey. I just want to hear your singing voice, that's all. Let's hear it." My reciprocated condescension wasn't as blatant.

"Not tonight," she responded.

She was winding me up. But I wasn't having it.

I sneered. "Not ever, sister. You're not capable."

This circular exchange went on and on, awkwardly. I wasn't sure why she continued to stick around and tell these bizarre lies. For what seemed like a lengthy amount of time, there were two sloppy lines of discussion taking place simultaneously: The first was whether or not Pre-Pubescent Thor should buy my book (he indicated that he wanted one but insisted on knowing more about it). The second revolved around how extremely important it was that we understood how popular the Doro lookalike was as a musical performer in Europe - despite the fact that there was zero proof of this stipulation, coupled with a blatant refusal to provide any.

During this chicanery, a third member of their group burst into the discussion. I wasn't sure where this guy was before (or where all of these peculiar folks were coming from randomly). This man was definitely not Nordic. He was short, paunchy, and had thinning black curly hair. Much older than the other two. His beady eyes reflected the neon Dos Equis sign on the wall behind me. His voice sounded American, with a proper command of English. He addressed everyone in an aggressive tone.

"Why would you buy this book? You don't need this!"

He looked at us dramatically, as if we were plotting to harvest his friend's kidneys or something. His beady little eyes were bloodshot and glassy as they strained to focus on my face. Tensions in the group returned to their earlier levels.

"No, no, I want to buy," came Thor Junior's reply. I wasn't sure why – dude could barely speak English, let alone read the language. I felt mildly sorry for him for some reason. He could *have* a copy, for crissakes. I didn't care.

The angry little curly-haired man spewed more invective and then stormed away, out through the front door of the bar. Doro followed him, walking backwards and watching us, lips puckered. It took some effort not to laugh. Then I looked over at the last member of this peculiar group. There was Emaciated Thor cutting a tragic figure, standing alone and swaying back and forth slightly, drunk off his Scandinavian ass.

"Can I still have book?" he mumbled.

"Here" I said, holding the book out to him. "Why don't you just take it?"

"No, here is money. I insist." He held up a crumpled American ten. "But only if you sign."

"Happy to do it."

I signed the front of the book and handed it to him. He passed the money to me and stumbled away.

Three months later I saw the copy on eBay, with my signature on the front cover. It was selling for three times the regular price and was billed as a rare collector's item. Seller's location – Norway.

$\backsim$

"I think you both should come up for a nightcap," I said to our gracious hosts.

Charlie and Lissa had been that and much more on this night. They had given us a glimpse into their lives, and now it was time to wind the evening down and invite them into ours for a while. Flemming was still in fine form, laughing and carrying on like a goddamn lunatic. It was maybe three in the morning. I wasn't sure what time our flight was the next day, but I believed it to be sometime later in the afternoon. If Flem didn't care, neither did I. We were living in the moment. It was all good.

We took our places once inside the room – Charlie and Lissa reclined together on one of the beds, Flemming on the other. I sat in a chair facing them. The television flickered with an MTV 'best of the

80s' countdown program, featuring D-list personalities presumably informed enough on the topic that their disposable commentary might be considered to be of value to whoever watches this stuff.

Our initial conversation was predictably sporadic and wildly carried out in unnecessarily raised volumes. After almost thirty minutes had passed the randomness had refined itself into more exploratory dialogue; the boldly unique kind that's powered by the lateness in hour. The kind during which everyone shows their cards.

Flem's halted, consistent bursts of mouth-breathing signaled to me that he had passed out before I even noticed that his eyes were closed. Lissa had also drifted off, curled up in the fetal position at Charlie's side. Now he and I were left to learn more about each other.

I was intrigued by Charlie's character. My understanding was that he was someone who had been on the inside of that machine that had so powerfully compelled me as an adolescent. He was *there*, on the other side, playing some part in it. He had been a fixture of the fabled Sunset Strip back in the day, having played with a guitarist that went on to achieve renown in hard rock and heavy metal circles with acts like Dio, and most recently serving as a member of the current Whitesnake lineup alongside David Coverdale himself. As Charlie and I talked, I made an effort to restrain as best I could any greedy compulsions that would lead to questions offered as self-serving forays: *Did you ever meet Nikki Sixx? Who else did you know back then? What was the Troubadour like? Impress me with something I've never heard before!*

I had been careful not to objectify him regardless of the degree of his involvement or his position on said involvement. He carried himself as a rock star would in terms of appearance and dress, and it would have been easy to get caught up in all of that and view him as a stereotype. The thing about Charlie though, was that he seemed rich in character. I was more interested to learn about him as a person beyond any imagined caricature.

Charlie spoke of his experiences with more or less the same essence that a soldier may have in recalling his time in Vietnam. There was very little ardour in his conveyance. He was almost a bit glib, a grizzled veteran who stripped away all of the saccharine and left only the bones. Charlie was certainly not interested in regaling me with lies and phony exaggerations about the people who used to be my heroes. He wasn't interested in a reaction, regardless of who he may or may not have known, or what his Sunset Strip involvement was back then. It went unclarified in our discussion.

"Listen man, we better get going." Charlie said to me as he roused his girlfriend. "*Lissa*. Time to go, Lissa."

I lifted myself out of the chair and past the black spots that formed in my eyes after I stood.

"Alright, man. Listen - thanks for everything, Charlie. I had a really great time tonight."

I was grateful to have met him and Lissa. We all stood and collectively looked at Flemming's sprawling frame, lifeless except for a very slight rise of his chest every three seconds.

"Tell Flem goodbye for us," Charlie said. "That guy should come with a warning label."

"I definitely will," I responded. "Take care of yourselves."

We exchanged meaningful hugs in commemoration of our shared time. I closed the door quietly behind them as they walked away.

$$\sim\!\!\mathfrak{O}$$

As I lay in the dark looking out the window at the lights that chased away Melbourne's nighttime, I recalled a concert I had been at in Toronto with Alison years ago. We noticed a woman who had to have been in her mid-fifties, posing for photos with a number of younger girls. The older woman was wearing skintight gold lamé pants, causing her to be instantly noticeable. Each member of this group of thirtysomething girls posed with this woman individually, striking stupid dramatic poses with their tongues out and hands extended forming devil horns gestures, being as visually ironic as they possibly could be. It seemed clear that these girls were conducting this impromptu photo session as a form of thinly-veiled mockery of this woman's appearance;

they were drunk and loutish, themselves dressed as hipsters (which meant they were all dressed the same).

The message I took away from this observation was that these girls intrinsically wanted to be associated with this expression somehow, but their understanding of (and allegiance to) societal constructs didn't allow for it. So, the girls deployed the convenient shield of irony to associate themselves with it instead – *hey, look at this silly caricature I'm with! In actuality I secretly want to be this person, but neither my social position nor my level of courage will permit it. This is close as I can get.*

After the girls walked away, the woman in gold lamé received a compliment on her pants from another concertgoer.

"Hey listen," she said in response. "There's a little bit of gold lamé pants in all of us."

Sixteen
Rural Mythology

"Where's my phone? I gotta find my fucking phone!"

For one incomprehensible moment, these words being shouted were infused into my dream, and a kaleidoscopic menagerie of images was instantly conjured up by my brain to make sense of them as best I cognitively could. But in dreams, at least in my dreams anyway, the walls seldom come together to form proper corners.

I opened my eyes. The sun felt warm on my face as my faculties slowly came together.

"I can't find my phone!" Flem exclaimed as he stood above me to confirm that he had successfully woken me up before continuing his scrambled search around the hotel room.

"Well, it's got to be somewhere," I mustered, snickering. I love that response. It was such an idiotic thing to say. Almost as annoying as responding, *well, where did you leave it?* People still say these things constantly. Older people in particular love using these responses. It's part of the geriatric lexicon. Like when older folks say, *what is the meaning of this?* Maybe I would give him that one next. He deserved it for yelling at me while I was sleeping.

"Thanks, you dick," he responded, moving the furniture around. "C'mon, get up and help me find it."

I had a very sharp headache that was incapacitating me at that moment. "Well Flem, where did you leave it?"

"If I knew where I left it, it wouldn't be lost!" Flem replied.

"You'd lose your head if it wasn't attached." Another geriatric gem.

"You're a fucking comedian this morning, eh?" Flem wasn't really angry. I could tell. He was still drunk. And just a little anxious about his phone being missing.

"I got a million of 'em, Flemming. I could go all day, I tell ya," I wheezed.

"That's because you're fucking old," he responded as he swung a pillow with both hands up from his ankles and over his head, crashing down on my face like he was chopping wood.

Bastard. My head was pounding.

"Now you're really on your own, you fucking ingrate." It actually really hurt.

I remained in a fetal position, squinting as I surveyed Flemming's continued attempts to locate his phone from the warm comfort of my bed. After a while I got up and helped him look. I just kinda walked around in circles, not terribly helpful at all.

"I'll phone Charlie and Lissa. Maybe it fell out of your pocket in their car," I said. I sent Charlie a message through Facebook instead explaining Flem's plight.

"*Ah-hahahahaha!*" Flem suddenly shrieked, holding up his Blackberry.

"Where was it?" I asked.

"Way under the bed. I have no idea how it got all the way under there."

I didn't either.

"Check our flight time. We should probably get going," I suggested.

Flem stared intently at his phone for a minute while his thumbs manipulated it. He looked up at me plaintively, tilting his head sideways.

"We missed it. The flight left an hour ago."

Fuck.

We sat down for a second and searched the floor for answers.

It was Friday. So, why not stick around sunny Florida for the time being? Sunshine was my friend, and even more so in crappy January. We decided to get a room in nearby Orlando and go from there.

Flem was in pre-Crystal mode. This meant he was still buzzed from the night before, capitalizing on the brief stay of execution before his imminent hangover set in. This phase of his recovery was always good for a few laughs. There would definitely be some hijinks in the next little while, just as surely as Arnold always really did know what Willis was talking about.

It didn't take long. After we had collected our things and headed downstairs to check out, we encountered a middle-aged guy in the elevator. Dude was a very, very big man. Likely had to iron his pants on the driveway. I braced for impact.

"*Hey!*" Flemming yelped at him. "I got a book for ya this morning. It's called *No Sleep 'Til Sudbury*. And it was written by this guy *right here!*" He shoved his finger in my face as he looked the man in the eye. "See? Look at the picture here. It's him! *See?*"

The man was very uncomfortable, having been unexpectedly stormed by Flemming in this way.

"No thanks," he said sheepishly, head down.

"Aw, *come on!* It's only twenty bucks! And I'm pretty sure I can get this guy to sign it for you too! What do you say? Autographed copy of *No Sleep 'Til Sudbury*, twenty bucks! You can't beat that with a bat!"

Nice Black Sheep reference, Flemming. He was an absolute spectacle. This poor man was wishing he had taken the stairs. Or stayed at the Hyatt.

The elevator door opened to the lobby.

"Give me your business card, in case you change your mind," Flem slurred. As this poor chap tried to get around him to escape, Flemming tripped and dropped my box of books in front of the elevator, scattering copies all over the lobby floor. The large man stepped over the pile and almost fell down in his haste to get away.

"Ah fuck, I dropped all the books! *Christ!*" Flem bellowed, carrying on like he was Jerry Lewis in full view of everyone in the lobby. People looked at him likely wondering if maybe he was one of the guys from *Jackass*. He was cackling like a fool. He got such a huge charge out of this.

We gathered up the books, stacking them in the box as they were previous to his Nutty Professor routine. After checking out, which took a great deal of time, we walked outside to the van. Flemming had calmed down considerably during the lengthy checkout. He asked for the keys.

"Are you kidding me?" I said.

"It's fine, seriously. It'll give me something to focus on," he said with a weak smirk.

"Here you go, Crystal."

In late afternoon we arrived in Orlando, land of women who possessed ridiculous shadows and people who were so good looking they seemed almost fictional. After fumbling our way through the return of the van and locating a hotel, Flemming and I finally got sorted at the Hilton Doubletree just off North Orange Avenue on the northern border of downtown Orlando. We crashed in our room, squandering precious Florida sunshine in favour of catching up on sleep.

Later, we would elect to stick around Orlando for the entire weekend to take in the city and make the most of the sun before heading back to the dismal Canadian winter that awaited us back home. I looked forward to a couple of lazy days without commitments of any kind.

But a brief period of decompression and reflection would come first. The tour was finished with now, and I felt like I needed to go back over the past week's experiences in my head and assess them all alongside each other for the meaning that needed to be made of them.

I lay down on my bed and closed my eyes, preventing myself from receiving the sun for the moment. I was tired, but sleep wouldn't come. My mind was lazy and sloppy, vacillating across a swirling wasteland of hazy memories and throwaway considerations. In poring over the events of the last few days, I thought about people and what motivated them to do the things they did. Samuel Johnson's quote floated through my mind among all of these thoughts – *'He who makes a beast of himself gets rid of the pain of being a man.'*

Alice in Chains' gloomy "Rooster" track came into my head, represented by former AIC frontman Layne Staley. "Rooster" howls with lonely blackness, and while I know the song was originally written about AIC guitar player Jerry Cantrell's father and his time spent fighting in the Vietnam War, the song's gloomy rage served as an ideal backdrop for Staley and his tortured mind. I wondered if Staley's predisposed acceptance of his own death while in the throes of his drug addiction made us like him more because of a perception that he didn't seem to fear death. In fact, he almost seemed to beckon it towards the end of his life. Maybe we lent his seemingly fearless figure greater power because of this, and maybe we used him as a prism in the commemoration of our own pain in the hopes of finding some form of artistry in it.

There was a point in my life where I wished that some of my musical heroes had died in a flourish of romantic affectation rather than devolve into pitiful, withered shells of what they formerly were, embarrassing themselves with silly commentary in documentaries fully intended to be entertaining mockery. It would have been better for them to burn out than to fade away. This was a selfish focus on my part, I know. I also know that I had simply chosen many of my heroes poorly as a young kid. The real heroes were the ones who survived their mistakes in doing it the wrong way, coming out the other end as survivors and better for it. It took me a long time to figure that out. Or at least to appreciate it. I thought about all of these things in consideration of my place in this, through the lens of my own contingencies.

I dwelled on some of the individuals I had experienced over the course of this trip who dealt with their own emotional pain using more passive-aggressive methods. The people who resisted growth and development to willingly stay behind as time moved forward. But it was important to make distinctions here, and not to make sweeping generalizations. I used to theorize that every woman who had large tattoos was trying to tell the world something she couldn't say with her mouth, and that it likely had to do with her relationship with Daddy. But it's easy to draw lazy conclusions. Additional discrepancy is always required.

A lot of the people I met this past week earned my respect for knowing themselves and staying true to what they believed in. They weren't trying to be someone else. I liked the fact that as illogical and maybe even ridiculous as it may have appeared to some, I had to respect the nobility with which these people lived their lives. It would be easy to label every one of them as leftover people who refused to accept the responsibilities of being an adult because they were afraid to deal with life. But this wasn't the case. I believed that I had seen far enough inside to learn that a lot of these people deserved respect for their perseverance. They were thoughtful, resilient folks who knew who they were, and I admired them for it.

My consideration of these sympathetic characters and their undying devotion to the cult of rock and roll in current day reminded me of the Greek mythological tale of Sisyphus. As punishment, Sisyphus was condemned to repeat the same meaningless task of pushing a boulder up a mountain only to have it roll back down again, for all of eternity. Sisyphus is what is referred to as an absurd hero, as his passion contributes directly to his torture in a neverending loop. His awareness of his plight is the root of the tragedy. If he thought he might actually succeed while the boulder rolled back down the mountain, the torment of his punishment would be diminished. But Sisyphus is *completely aware* of the scope of his own misery. And that's the point – it's this clear understanding of his destiny that makes it possible for his torment to be his happiness.

The tragic moment in Sisyphus' plight is when the boulder begins its descent back down the mountain, right after it was just pushed all the way up. It's during this moment that Sisyphus truly realizes his tragic position, and this is the crux of his intended punishment. When he comes to grips with the futility of this task and the permanence of his fate, only then can he finally realize the absurdity of his situation and develop an acceptance of it. The critical aspect here is that this exercise was originally intended to be punishment through never end-ing frustration. But - there was quiet, satisfying nobility in the work, which negated any punishment or frustration. Simply making a con-sistent, valiant effort with purpose justifies the task regardless of the outcome, or even the perception of the outcome for that matter. Absurd heroism. This concept was exactly what I had witnessed in the flesh this past week.

From the bed in my Orlando hotel room, I imagined that there was a certain virtue in the insistence to press on in a post-rock and roll America. The outcome wasn't important. It was the will and the integ-rity that warranted respect.

Epilogue

As I sat waiting at a table by the window in the mildly swishy *Ellven* restaurant in downtown Toronto, I looked forward to seeing my dear childhood friend Bryan Sloss. He had selected *Ellven* as the location where we would have dinner before heading into the nearby Air Canada Centre to see the recently reunited (though sans Bill Ward) Black Sabbath.

Important summer sunlight shone down on me through the window as I looked around at my fellow patrons. Plenty of sales types in nice suits, lying to each other in boisterous bullshit conversations held over the clinking of glasses and laughter that had been well practiced. To my right, outside the window, were metalheads of various description. Some of them were young but most were much older, donning concert tees from yesteryear and plodding along like soldiers towards their battlefield. Their long unkempt hair was blowing behind them like unfortunate flags identifying a melancholy purpose.

And here I was, perfectly square in the middle. Again. As I always had been.

My pal appeared at the table.

"*Hey! How you doin', man?*" Sloss beamed with a bright smile. I rose up from my seat to greet him.

"Doing great. Good to see you."

He settled into his chair in front of me. As always, he was crisply dressed, looking clean and fit. He had the professional sheen that I felt like he would have when we were kids, back when we sat next to each other through so many high school classes. He was ambitious and he'd persevered to get to where he was today. He was an achiever, and he could be proud of that. It hadn't been easy for either of us. We had taken different roads, and we both had difficulty getting from there to here. We were good for each other back then and even better for each other now.

Whenever we sat down together, the conversation typically harkened back to our younger lives. We both recognized and respected the importance of this commemoration. We pulled vague shapes from our memories and puzzles emerged, one of us filling in the missing pieces that the other had forgotten. Many times the puzzles were left incomplete.

"I'd love to watch a video of my teenage life from start to finish, just to be able to fill in those little gaps," Sloss said.

"Wouldn't want to live it all over again?" I asked dryly. I knew what the answer would be.

"Lord, no!" came his response. "But I'd love to have that closure, y'know?"

I did know. I knew that it might make us a bit more complete as the people who sat in front of each other on this day. Not necessarily better people, just more complete. There had been times when I felt like there were gaps I needed to fill by going back to where we grew up. I had walked the streets of our hometown, trying to find things that were no longer there. I don't do it anymore, but sometimes I still hear that din that's left behind by something missing. We both did.

We both knew that seeing Black Sabbath would be a small measure of going back there; just as it was when we saw Judas Priest, and Slash with Myles Kennedy, and all of the other concerts we went to together in the past three or four years. I felt comfortable being in this position at these shows now, but I wasn't sure I would initially. I had felt some form of transformative pride. It had been almost thirty years since we had seen Iron Maiden together as mulleted teenage metalheads. Going back there was therapeutic in an indescribable way.

There was a difference between going back there and *being* there. But that was the hardest part to delineate. Being there meant you had stayed there, or would remain there. But maybe wanting to go back there meant you *should have* stayed there, and that you were suppressing some need to do that. Lying to yourself.

On the other side of the window, a man who looked to be in his late forties wearing a Maiden Japan sleeveless tee with stringy hair reaching halfway down his back walked by. His arms were embossed with massive Ozzy Osbourne and Black Sabbath tattoos among other obvious heavy metal imagery. Sloss and I both watched as he trudged past.

"What's the difference between that guy, and us?" I asked.

"He stayed back there."

"Is he stuck, or does he just not want to move?"

"*Ca-an he-e se-e or is he blind?*" Sloss responded. I laughed.

This quip was more than just timely on this night. It carried a deeper significance here. The individual described in the lyrics of Black Sabbath's "Iron Man", the song from which Sloss had borrowed this line, shared significant similarities with what the average metalhead is perceived to be – a misunderstood character ostracized by society. The "Iron Man" lyrics portray their subject as a tragic figure with a somewhat more grandiose flaw, but I always interpreted them as a metaphor for the heavy metal outcast. The "Iron Man" and the diehard heavy metal devotee are practically one and the same.

"Some people don't want to acknowledge forward movement. They don't want to accept the passing of time. Maybe because they're afraid."

"Of what?"

"Of *life*."

We knew that we both had a lot more in common with that guy than a lot of folks might believe. This both frightened and delighted me during the times I considered it.

"You know what the difference between us and that guy is?" I said, holding up my hand with thumb and forefinger extended, as if holding an imaginary shot glass between them. "It's *this*."

But the real question was what constituted this space between my fingers, and whether or not it was justified. I verbalized this question, even if neither of us wanted that to happen.

"But what's *in here*?"

Sloss looked at me wordlessly for a moment, with an expression I had often seen on his face back in eleventh grade chemistry all those years ago. There was a hint of a smile in his eyes, despite the fact that one would not appear on his mouth. He turned his gaze down to his steak, working through it with gleaming utensils. No answer.

There is no answer.

These are just things we think about.